The Ultimate Guidebook for Adults With ADHD

Steps to Conquer and Unleash Your Potential with Insights, Strategies, and Techniques for Coping and Thriving for a Better Life!

Chelsi Parrill

Contents

Introduction

Hello, my name is Chelsi Parrill, and I am the author here to share my journey with you in this book. Living with ADHD has been a constant in my life, though it wasn't until my late 20s that I became aware of its presence and impact on my daily activities. When I finally received my diagnosis, my immediate response was to seek a solution, and I turned to my doctors with a pressing question: "How do I get rid of it?"

At that point in my life, I was under the impression that ADHD was a condition that could be simply cured or fixed. I envisioned a variety of potential remedies, from taking a prescribed pill for a set duration to altering my diet in significant ways. I was ready and willing to take whatever steps necessary to eliminate the challenges ADHD presented in my life. However, I soon learned that ADHD is a lifelong condition, a revelation that began a new chapter in my understanding of myself and how to navigate the world around me.

Growing up, I was perplexed and frustrated by my consistent difficulty maintaining a clean and orderly room despite my genuine desire to achieve just that. I remember the numerous occasions where this struggle would land me in trouble, leaving me feeling inadequate and unable to measure up to the standards set by my sister. She seemed to embody organization effortlessly; she never misplaced her belongings and always knew exactly where everything was.

In stark contrast, I would find myself in my room, overwhelmed by emotions and crying after losing items that held great importance to me. I would firmly tell myself, "This time will be different; I will put this in a safe spot." However, my ADHD played a pivotal role in sabotaging these well-intentioned plans. I would place the item in a safe spot, but my pervasive lack of organization would result in other things piled on top of it. Eventually, the item would get lost amidst the clutter, leading to an endless cycle of frustration and disappointment.

Some of these lost items were never found, despite the strenuous efforts and unwavering support of my dear mother, a beautiful soul who stood by me through thick and thin. She poured her love and patience into helping me search for my misplaced treasures, demonstrating unmatched care and dedication.

As time passed, the challenges associated with my ADHD did not fade; instead, they seemed to intensify. From a young age, I grappled with anger outbursts, mood swings, and difficulty calming down after being upset. The emotional strain was palpable, not just for me but also for those closest to me.

As I grew older, I became more aware of my actions and words impact on others, particularly my mother and sister, who bore the brunt of my outbursts. They were my only family, my constant support, yet I noticed the toll my behavior took on them. Deep down, I knew something was amiss: a part of me seemed beyond my control. These fits of anger and the inability to think things through before acting or speaking left a trail of emotional upheaval.

I often sought solace and forgiveness in the aftermath, overwhelmed by guilt and the need to make amends. I'd go to my mother and sister, tears streaming down my face, offering heartfelt apologies. Yet, as they rightly pointed out, an apology could not undo the words spoken or the pain inflicted, no matter how sincere. "You can apologize all you want, but the damage is done, and you can't take it back," they would say.

Remarkably, despite the hurt I caused, they found it within themselves to forgive me, usually within a few hours or less. Looking back, I am immensely grateful for their forgiveness and understanding, recognizing that not everyone is fortunate enough to have such a supportive and compassionate family.

Now that I am older and have had time to reflect on my past, I can recognize that exercise played a significant role in mitigating the symptoms of my ADHD and tempering my outbursts. However, at the time, I was oblivious to the fact that I had ADHD, and consequently, I remained unaware of why exercise seemed to bring me a sense of calm and stability.

Unbeknownst to me, the exercise served as a natural outlet for my pent-up energy and frustration, helping to regulate my mood and emotions. The physical activity provided a much-needed break for my overactive mind, allowing me to reset and find balance.

Embarking on the journey of marriage and motherhood, I remained in the dark about my ADHD. Even after experiencing a stroke, a life-altering event I plan to delve into in a future book, my ADHD went undiagnosed and unacknowledged. It wasn't until a few years after the birth of my second child that the puzzle pieces finally started to come together, illuminating the ADHD that had been affecting me all along.

My emotional outbursts, organizational chaos, numerous unfinished projects, and impulsive actions - whether engaging in risky behaviors or succumbing to impulsive spending - were all indicators pointing towards ADHD. My husband stood steadfastly by my side through all these tumultuous times, showcasing a strength and resilience that can only be described as extraordinary. His unwavering support and love were my pillars of strength, helping me navigate the challenging waters of undiagnosed ADHD.

He is a diamond in the rough, a testament to the power of love, patience, and understanding. His golden heart saw past the struggles and embraced me for who I am, ADHD and all.

Despite the strong bond and mutual support my husband and I share, our journey together has not been without its challenges and turbulent moments. Navigating life with undiagnosed ADHD added complexity to our relationship, manifesting in miscommunications, emotional outbursts, and impulsive decisions. These dynamics occasionally led to friction and misunderstandings, testing the resilience of our partnership. However, the rough patches also served as opportunities for growth and deepened understanding. Together, we learned to navigate the stormy waters and, in the process, forged a stronger, more resilient bond. His patience, combined with a willingness to understand the intricacies of ADHD, played a pivotal role in overcoming these challenges and solidifying the foundation of our marriage.

In sharing my story through this book, I hope to illuminate the complexities of living with ADHD, mainly how it can manifest in various aspects of one's life, including relationships and parenting. My journey to diagnosis was a long and winding road, filled with challenges but moments of profound realization and growth.

My sincerest wish is that my experiences, shared candidly on these pages, will offer solace, understanding, and a sense of community to others who may find themselves on a similar path. Living with ADHD is a unique journey, but it does not have to be walked alone.

Now, as we launch into the heart of this book, we embark on a shared journey of discovery and understanding about ADHD. Through these pages, we'll explore the multifaceted nature of this condition, shedding light on its challenges and the unique strengths it can bestow.

We'll navigate through personal anecdotes, skillful insights, and practical strategies to demystify ADHD and foster a more profound comprehension of its impacts on daily life. From unraveling the complexity of managing emotions and maintaining relationships to mastering organization and embracing the creative bursts that ADHD can bring, we will cover it all.

Our exploration will not just stop at understanding the condition; we'll also inquire into coping mechanisms, tools, and techniques that can enhance quality of life. We'll learn about the power of routine, mindfulness benefits, and the crucial role of support networks in managing ADHD.

Whether you're an individual living with ADHD, a loved one seeking to understand and support, or simply a curious mind, this book aims to be a resource, a companion, and a catalyst for change. So, let's turn the page, keep an open mind, and discover the many facets of ADHD together, unraveling the mysteries and embracing the journey with courage, knowledge, and hope.

Chapter 1

Embracing ADHD and Neurodiversity

Let's start this book with a foundational understanding: ADHD and neurodiversity aren't swear words or as taboo to talk about as in the past. More and more people, like myself, learn about it in their adulthood, whether they're diagnosed with it, know about loved ones who are, or advocate for normalizing the conversation around it.

By learning to embrace these differences in the brain and how they affect adults in their daily lives, we help create a more knowledgeable and understanding community. At the same time, when you learn to accept the diagnoses (of yourself or someone else), you empower yourself to create a better, more fulfilling life for everyone involved.

Of course, to embrace something, you first have to understand it. As I mentioned, all those childhood years where I felt different from my sibling but didn't understand why made me feel inadequate. And you've likely felt (or are still feeling) the same way. However, when you learn what ADHD is, understand neurodiversity, and know how to recognize the symptoms, you're already on your way to embracing it as a whole.

In this chapter, we will dive into the brilliance and beauty of the ADHD and neurodiverse brain. It's not a disability; it's a superpower. And embracing the diagnosis means you have a catalyst for positive change. Let's take Alex, for example. He is a 32-year-old professional navigating the challenges of undiagnosed ADHD.

Alex struggled with deadlines, was disorganized at work, and found maintaining healthy relationships challenging. His life took a positive turn after receiving the ADHD diagnosis, arming him with newfound clarity. Along with mental health professionals, he started with mindfulness practices, used organizational tools, and partook in physical activity to improve his quality of life.

Alex's transformation led to improved work performance, a promotion, and even a long-term, committed relationship. By embracing his neurodiversity, he found a supportive community and lived a more fulfilling life. This is only one example, and yours is certainly not the same. However, Alex's story is one of hope: through acceptance and self-love, ADHD and neurodiversity don't become a roadblock but a map to a better future.

Unpacking ADHD

All this talk about ADHD might have you wondering what it means. So, let's start with ADHD: it is short for Attention Deficit Hyperactivity Disorder. It is essentially a neurological condition that affects about 11% of children and 5% of adults in the United States (ADDitude Editors, 2017).

It affects the brain's executive functions, including self-control, working memory, the ability to focus, and flexible thinking. Think about it this way: it affects your everyday life in ways neurotypical people (those without cognitive differences) don't understand. It will clean your room, but you will become distracted.

It's hyper-focusing on projects and forgetting to eat, shower, or do other things on your to-do list. It's not replying to a text someone sent a week ago and ignoring all incoming messages because you feel too guilty about missing the first one. Finally, it's going into an online shopping frenzy to chase that influx of dopamine (the pleasure and motivation hormone).

It can also include a whole host of other symptoms in adults, including the following:

- "Often being late or forgetting things,
- Anxiety,
- Low self-esteem,
- Problems at work,
- Trouble controlling anger,
- Impulsiveness,

- Substance misuse or addiction,
- Trouble staying organized,
- Procrastination,
- Easily frustrated,
- Often bored,
- Trouble concentrating when reading,
- Mood swings,
- Depression, or
- Relationship problems" (WebMD Editorial Contributors, 2022).

If you experience some or all of these symptoms, chances are that you might have ADHD (of course, a medical professional needs to make the diagnosis to be sure). And if you have it (or think you do), you might have experienced common misconceptions or myths about the condition. These mistruths make it challenging to discern what you should believe, feel, and do about it.

With different types of narratives out there, it's best to tackle these myths about ADHD head-on to help you accept and embrace it. Amanda Morin, a neurodiversity and educational consultant, busts some common misconceptions about ADHD.

- **Myth 1: "ADHD isn't a 'real' condition."** Not only is it a medical condition, a difference in how the brain develops, but studies show that one in four people with ADHD has a parent with the same diagnosis.

- **Myth 2: "People with ADHD just need to try harder."** It has nothing to do with focus, motivation, or laziness. An ADHD brain functions differently because it's structured differently.
- **Myth 3: "People with ADHD can't" ever focus."** People with ADHD do have trouble staying focused on some tasks, yes, but it's not always a lack of focus. Sometimes, hyper-focusing on tasks happens as well. That's when you focus intensely on something for prolonged periods and can't shift concentration to something else.
- **Myth 4: "All people with ADHD are hyperactive."** Although the H stands for Hyperactivity, it doesn't always manifest as jumping around or being unable to sit still. In some, it could be needing to move constantly, for example, tapping your finger while working, playing with your hair, or fumbling with a fidget gadget. In others, the hyperactive part merely presents as taking on more tasks than they can complete. Of course, you do get those who don't get hyperactive at all; then, we refer to the condition as ADD (Attention Deficit Disorder).
- **Myth 5: "Only boys and men have ADHD."** While it is twice as likely for men to get an ADHD diagnosis, women get it, too. Unfortunately, this stigma means misdiagnosis of teen girls and adult women who have the symptoms but get mislabeled as anxious or depressed.

- **Myth 6: "ADHD is a learning disability."**
  ADHD isn't in itself a learning disability, but it can
  make it difficult to absorb new knowledge. That's
  because the brain's executive functions don't work like
  others. Boredom, impulsiveness, forgetfulness, and
  trouble concentrating mean it takes longer to learn
  something. Someone with ADHD doesn't have a
  learning disability; they have trouble staying focused
  and entertained long enough for learning to take
  place (Morin, n.d.).

The Weight of Neurodiversity

Now that we understand ADHD in more detail, let's look at
neurodiversity. Harvard Health says it describes the different
ways people interact with and experience the world around
them (Baumer & Frueh, 2021). It's not a defect; it's just a brain
that works differently than others.

Although neurodiversity describes a brain that forms and functions differently, it's an umbrella term. It describes individuals
with trouble concentrating, communication struggles, and
compromised fine motor skills. Sounds familiar? Well, it should
because ADHD and Autism Spectrum Disorder fall under the
neurodivergent umbrella. And like ADHD, it isn't a belittling
term but one of empowerment.

The neurodiversity movement was initiated by Judy Singer, an
advocate on the autism spectrum who wanted social justice for
neurodivergent people (Miller, 2023). She started it to chal-

lenge the stigma that neurodiversity is a deficit. Instead, she redefined it as "neurological minorities."

By taking away the negative narrative around neurodiversity, we emphasize the strengths associated with these conditions. You can probably name a few, like increased creativity, empathy, curiosity, etc. So, instead of focusing on the weaknesses, we look at neurodiversity from a strength-based perspective. It becomes a therapeutic approach where you can recognize your unique abilities instead of focusing on your perceived shortcomings.

If more people adopt this way of thinking about neurodiverse conditions like ADHD, society will become a better place. That's because it challenges environments that weren't as inclusive for people with differences in the past. Think about schools or the workplace, for example. How did they accommodate the differences in brain processing for neurodiverse people? Being an adult with ADHD (or knowing a few who have it), you might remember some of the following scenarios:

- A rigid classroom structure where the lack of flexibility and movement worsened their focus, leading to frustration and a decline in academic performance.
- A lack of clear instructions hindered their ability to organize tasks and prioritize assignments, leading to missed deadlines and heightened anxiety.
- Limited or short breaks were insufficient for them to recharge and refocus, resulting in increased stress and feeling overwhelmed.

- Open-office environments made it challenging to concentrate amid constant visual and auditory distractions.
- Strict attendance policies caused a rise in ADHD-related difficulties in time management, occasionally resulting in tardiness despite sincere efforts.

Luckily, now that we can recognize neurodiversity as a part of society, we help create more inclusive environments where everyone can flourish, no matter how their brains function. Changing from seeing neurodivergent conditions as disorders to differences is instrumental in creating a more inclusive and less stigmatized society. Less stigma leads to an appreciation of diverse cognitive styles and more people fulfilling their true potential.

The Benefits of a Neurodiverse Society

A neurodiverse society means there is no stigma, only opportunities. It's a society where you can flourish, no matter your diagnosis. While it benefits the person with the diagnosis, society benefits from it, too. Let's look at some benefits of a neurodiverse society and data to back up the claims:

1. **Enhanced Problem Solving:** Neurodivergent software-testing teams at Hewlett Packard Enterprise (HPE) were observed to be 30% more productive than others (Mio, 2023).
2. **Increased Creativity:** Neurodivergent individuals often bring a unique and innovative perspective to

creativity. Thanks to neurodiversity programs, remarkable breakthroughs have been achieved, such as a groundbreaking technical solution valued at approximately $40 million at Systems, Applications & Products in Data Processing(SAP) (Austin & Pisano, 2017).

3. **Greater Innovation:** Companies that have implemented neurodiversity programs, like SAP, have experienced many benefits beyond just enhancing their reputation. These benefits include better productivity and a boost in innovative capabilities (Austin & Pisano, 2017).

4. **A Positive Impact on Company Culture:** Embracing neurodiversity creates an inclusive environment where each employee's unique abilities are valued. Companies, such as HPE, have witnessed increased employee engagement in areas influenced by neurodiversity programs (Mio, 2023).

5. **Inclusive Environment:** Neurodiversity programs positively change the corporate mindset, fostering a more inclusive environment. SAP has set a goal to make 1% of its workforce neurodiverse by 2020, acknowledging diversity's immense value (Austin & Pisano, 2017).

6. **Shared Values:** A neurodiverse workforce strengthens the sense of community within the company. SAP's neurodiversity program has placed over 100 participants in 18 roles, challenging assumptions about job roles for neurodivergent individuals (Austin & Pisano, 2017).

7. **Educational Initiatives:** Educational initiatives play a crucial role in raising awareness. Did you know that the Centers for Disease Control and Prevention says autism in the United States is 2% in boys and 0,5% in girls (Stanton, 2023)?

8. **Recruitment and Hiring Practices:** Adapting recruitment and hiring processes is crucial. Companies like HPE are collaborating with universities to enhance the identification and access of neurodiverse talent (Mio, 2023).

9. **Workplace Accommodations:** It's essential to prioritize providing necessary accommodations. Many neurodiverse individuals require workplace adjustments, like noise-canceling headphones, to fully utilize their abilities (Stanton, 2023).

10. **Diversity and Inclusion Policies:** Incorporating neurodiversity into diversity and inclusion policies shows a firm commitment. Companies like Microsoft strive to make mainstream talent processes more friendly toward neurodiversity (Mio, 2023).

11. **Mentoring and Support Networks:** Establishing mentoring programs and support networks is crucial. SAP has introduced two "support circles" encompassing workplace and personal life. These circles provide mentors, coaches, and buddies specifically for neurodiverse employees (Austin & Pisano, 2017).

Although many of these statistics are based on single companies, they're not exclusive. When we come together as a society and include the neurodivergent narrative, we all benefit from it. More inclusivity means less stigmatization and more fulfilled potential.

Recognizing the Symptoms

When you think about ADHD and its symptoms, what comes to mind first? For many, it might be the image of a hyperactive child not knowing how to calm down. Or it could be the teenager with difficulties studying for the agonizingly boring history test. But that's not always the case for adults with ADHD. So, let's challenge the stereotype and focus on the symptoms adults might have:

- Impulsive behavior and decision-making
- Challenges in organization and task prioritization
- Ineffective time management skills
- Difficulty maintaining focus on a specific task
- Struggles with multitasking
- Restlessness and excessive activity
- Poor planning abilities
- Low tolerance for frustration
- Frequent mood swings
- Difficulty completing tasks and follow-through
- Tendency to have a quick temper
- Challenges in coping with stress
- Carelessness and lack of attention to detail
- Initiating new tasks before completing existing ones

- Limited organizational skills
- Inability to focus or prioritize effectively
- Regularly misplacing or losing items
- Forgetfulness
- Restlessness and edginess
- Struggling to remain quiet and talking out of turn
- Impulsive responses, including interrupting others
- Mood swings, irritability, and quick temper
- Struggling to deal with stress effectively
- Extreme impatience
- Engaging in risky activities with little consideration for personal or others' safety, such as reckless driving (Mayo Clinic, 2023).

If you experience some or all of these symptoms, chances are it significantly impacts how you (or the person with the symptoms) cope. That's because the symptoms can manifest in various areas of life, including work, relationships, and personal growth.

What do I mean by that? Let me explain: adults with ADHD don't necessarily have parents who understand and meet their needs. Nor do they have help navigating the neurotypically inclined world. And although they might have partners who are willing to learn, the symptoms still affect their lives in various ways, like the following:

1. Disorganization:

In the workplace, individuals with ADHD may face difficulties with organizational skills, which can make it challenging for them to keep track of tasks and prioritize them effectively. As a result, they may experience missed deadlines, confusion, and decreased overall efficiency. Just picture a professional who frequently misplaces important documents, struggles to prioritize tasks, and consistently misses crucial project deadlines due to disorganization.

2. Relationship Concerns:

ADHD traits, such as inattentiveness, quickly getting bored, and talking over others, can strain professional, romantic, or platonic relationships. These traits may create a perception of insensitivity, irresponsibility, or uncaring behavior. In a romantic relationship, a partner with ADHD may unintentionally appear disinterested or inattentive, leading to misunderstandings and emotional strain.

3. Lack of Focus:

The main symptom of ADHD, which is a lack of focus, extends beyond simply having trouble paying attention. It involves being easily distracted, finding it challenging to listen during conversations, missing essential details, and struggling to finish tasks or projects. Picture someone in a business meeting constantly getting sidetracked, having difficulty concentrating on meaningful discussions, and missing crucial details that affect decision-making.

4. Restlessness and Anxiety:

Restlessness is a common trait associated with ADHD, and it can often lead to frustration and anxiety, especially when immediate action is not possible. This anxiety can have an impact on both personal and professional aspects of life. For instance, individuals with ADHD may feel restless and anxious in a sedentary office environment, which can result in a constant need to move or fidget as a way to cope with their internal restlessness.

5. Emotional Concerns:

ADHD can affect your emotional well-being because it can make you look for impulsive excitement when feeling bored. Even minor frustrations can become overwhelming, affecting mood and potentially leading to feelings of depression. Imagine someone going through sudden mood swings, finding it difficult to cope with minor setbacks at work, and facing challenges in maintaining emotional stability.

And although ADHD symptoms affect many adults' lives in various ways, it also affects the internal nature of those individuals. It means that the symptoms affect your psychological and emotional experiences in your everyday life. Here are some examples from WebMD (Ellis, 2022):

1. **Compulsive Eating:** Individuals with ADHD may turn to compulsive eating as a means to temporarily elevate dopamine levels, seeking the pleasure associated with heightened brain activity.
2. **Anxiety:** The continual on-edge sensation may stem from ADHD symptoms, and addressing ADHD can have a positive impact on anxiety levels.
3. **Substance Misuse:** The impulsive tendencies leading to overeating can also contribute to risky behaviors like substance misuse, establishing a potential connection between ADHD and substance use disorders.
4. **Chronic Stress:** Stress linked to ADHD may result in muscle tension, breathing problems, heart issues, difficulties controlling blood sugar, and digestive problems.
5. **Sleep Problems:** Disruption of the circadian rhythm makes it difficult for you to fall asleep and wake up regularly, impacting overall sleep quality.
6. **Employment Problems:** Meeting workplace expectations becomes challenging, potentially leading to difficulties maintaining employment.
7. **Trouble With Deadlines:** Individuals with ADHD may grapple with time management, resulting in challenges meeting work, school, and personal project deadlines.
8. **Impulsive Spending:** Uncontrolled impulsive spending can lead to financial strain, with a drained bank account or damaged credit.

9. **Financial Issues:** Managing tasks like keeping up with paper statements and the checkbook becomes challenging when ADHD symptoms are not under control.
10. **Screen Addiction:** The constant change of images and stimuli on screens provides a reward for the ADHD brain, making it challenging to disengage from electronic devices.

Looking at the list of symptoms and how they affect your life, externally and internally, it's no wonder you might feel alone! And what makes it worse is that ADHD in adulthood often goes undiagnosed or misdiagnosed. But why does that happen, exactly? Well, the American Psychological Association (Fairbank, 2023) has some ideas:

Firstly, the presence of co-existing conditions that mimic ADHD symptoms can complicate the diagnostic process. At the same time, the lack of early treatment for ADHD, combined with its symptoms, can cause other conditions to surface, like anxiety and depression, which suppress the root cause: ADHD.

Of course, there is an overlap between ADHD and other conditions, like autism spectrum disorder, which adds complexity. And let's not forget to mention the onset of symptoms in layers, with ADHD emerging after developmental disorders, which makes it even more challenging. Finally, the persistence of ADHD symptoms, in contrast to the precise nature of anxiety and depression, can lead to overlooking the underlying condition.

When we look at these factors, we understand that symptoms vary depending on specific conditions for each person; it is no wonder why it is difficult to diagnose ADHD in adults accurately. It's even more understandable why many adults with ADHD learned to mask their symptoms with various coping mechanisms.

When an adult has ADHD, they often develop coping mechanisms to "mask" their symptoms. They do that by behaving in ways they think they should, and it can be both healthy and unhealthy. It can be a way to navigate social expectations and avoid shame and ridicule. For example, these coping mechanisms or masking techniques could include the following:

- staying quiet to avoid talking too much,
- obsessively checking belongings to prevent losing items,
- reacting in expected ways rather than expressing your true feelings,
- hiding Hyperactivity through calmness,
- excessively organizing to compensate for memory issues,
- suppressing stemming behaviors to avoid disturbing others and
- appearing "fine" while struggling internally.

While these can initially be helpful, they can become challenging to manage over time. These strategies, aimed at fitting in and managing daily life, can lead to shame and guilt as you strive to appear in control and accepted by others.

If this sounds like you (or someone you know), consider seeking a professional evaluation. Knowing for sure whether you or your friend are diagnosed with ADHD will help you get a better understanding of the lived experiences and explore potential support and strategies.

Activity: Reflecting on ADHD Perceptions

1. List three things you know about ADHD right now.

1. _____

2. _____

3. _____

2. Explore the chapter for insights into ADHD from real examples and expert opinions.

_____

_____

_____

_____

_____

_____

3. Revisit your initial list after absorbing the information.

_____

_____

_____

_____

4. Reflect on how your views may have changed or been validated.

_____

_____

_____

_____

5. Take note of specific insights gained about ADHD masking, diagnosis difficulties, and internal symptoms.

_____

_____

_____

_____

Now that you've challenged your perceptions about ADHD, I'd like to end this chapter by introducing you to Sarah. She is a 35-year-old professional navigating a chaotic office and struggling in personal relationships. Unaware of her ADHD, deadlines loomed like storms, projects faltered, and social connections strained. Each day, she brought confusion, leaving her feeling different and eroding her self-esteem. Little did Sarah know that an ADHD diagnosis awaited, promising clarity, effective coping strategies, and improved relationships.

Sarah's lack of knowledge about her ADHD brought emotional turmoil, fostering feelings of inadequacy and straining relationships. Practically, it translated into a chaotic work environment where deadlines felt insurmountable, and opportunities slipped away. The absence of understanding amplified daily struggles, creating a cycle of frustration and self-doubt.

Sarah's "Aha moment" came when, after years of confusion and setbacks, she sought professional help. The ADHD diagnosis was a revelation, explaining the challenges that had long perplexed her. Understanding her brain's unique wiring became pivotal, bringing clarity to a once bewildering journey.

Post-diagnosis, Sarah's life underwent a profound transformation. Armed with self-awareness, she navigated daily challenges with a newfound understanding of her ADHD. Embracing her neurodiversity fostered better relationships as loved ones started to understand and embrace the intricacies of her mind. Coping strategies tailored to her unique strengths replaced futile attempts to conform. The diagnosis catalyzed positive change, leading Sarah to a more fulfilling and empowered life.

Chapter 2

The Road to Diagnosis and Building Resilience

Have you ever found yourself missing deadlines, losing focus, or struggling to control your emotions and wondered, "Is it just me?" You're about to embark on a journey that could connect the dots and show you that it could be ADHD. And that's okay. Let's explore how to recognize the signs, get diagnosed, and build emotional strength to live your best life.

In this chapter, you will learn some essential steps to an ADHD diagnosis and how to navigate the challenges. From recognizing the signs that may have gone unnoticed to understanding the diagnostic process, you will unravel the complexities surrounding ADHD in adults. You'll also explore strategies for building emotional resilience, providing the tools to embrace your neurodiversity and live a more fulfilling life. Let's get started, shall we? Let's explore the journey toward diagnosis and the transformative power of building resilience.

Spotting the Signs for Diagnosis

In chapter one, you unpacked ADHD and learned to recognize the symptoms. But, like most diagnoses, ADHD symptoms aren't a one-size-fits-all type of thing. Some signs usually suggest that a person might have ADHD, while others are more obvious. And then other conditions can manifest alongside ADHD, making it more challenging to diagnose. So, let's dive into these varying symptoms so you know how to look for the signs.

Signs Usually Suggesting You Have ADHD

Here's a quick list of signs that might suggest someone has ADHD, though it's important to remember these can also be due to other factors. A professional diagnosis is needed to confirm ADHD:

- Getting sidetracked by less crucial tasks.
- Difficulty focusing and frequent daydreaming.
- Organizational issues leading to chronic lateness.
- Challenges starting and finishing projects.
- Forgetting appointments and losing items.
- Impulsive speaking and interrupting others.
- Reckless actions and limited self-control.
- Easily stressed, flustered, and irritable.
- Short temper and emotional management issues.
- Restlessness and a constant search for excitement.
- Struggles to sit still and maintain attention.

- Challenges in work and relationships, possibly with substance misuse.

Common signs in most adults with ADHD include:

- Not paying attention to details.
- Making careless mistakes.
- Being easily distracted.
- Incomplete tasks.
- Forgetfulness.
- Frequently switching tasks.
- Daydreaming.
- Impulsive actions.
- Excessive talking.
- Losing or forgetting items (One Bright Mental Health, 2023).

If these sound familiar, it's possible you might have ADHD. Remember, ADHD can coexist with other conditions, so getting a professional evaluation is crucial for a clear understanding.

How ADHD Can Manifest Alongside Other Conditions

People with undiagnosed ADHD often think it's something else because ADHD frequently hangs out with other conditions, a scenario known as comorbidity. It's like ADHD is part of a complex band of life challenges. In fact, about 60% to

80% of the time, ADHD comes with these co-stars, making things more intricate (Mentalhelp.net, 2019).

Here's a quick rundown of ADHD's frequent companions:

- **Oppositional Defiant Disorder (ODD)**: Present in 21% to 60% of those with ADHD, it's like adding a rebellious streak to the mix.
- **Depression**: Found in 10% to 30% of ADHD folks, this isn't your typical depression but more an impulsive, high-energy mood mix.
- **Anxiety Disorders**: About 25% of people with ADHD also have anxiety, making for a mix of mood swings and restless energy.
- **Bipolar Disorder**: This joins the ADHD party in about half of men and a quarter of women, adding intense emotions to the mix.
- **Conduct Disorder**: Seen in 25% to 40% of hyperactive ADHD kids, it brings a wild, rule-breaking energy.
- **Learning Disorder**: Over half of ADHD adults struggle with learning disorders, adding a twist to the educational journey.
- **Substance Misuse**: Sometimes, ADHD parties with substances like alcohol and marijuana, not always following the rules.
- **Autism Spectrum Disorders**: There's some overlap with ADHD, but autism adds unique social and communication challenges (Mentalhelp.net, 2019).

Understanding this mix is key to finding the right moves for managing ADHD and its diverse group of friends. Let's learn to dance to this intricate playlist!

ADHD Symptoms Checklist

Below is a list of all the signs, symptoms, and comorbid conditions discussed in this chapter. Encircle or highlight all the signs you experience. The more you relate with them, the higher the chances are that you have ADHD.

My ADHD Signs and Symptoms Checklist:

- Sidetracked easily
- Focus challenges
- Daydreaming
- Organizational issues
- Project initiation troubles
- Impulsive speaking/actions
- Limited self-control
- Stress and irritability
- Short temper, low self-esteem
- Emotional struggles, motivation
- Restlessness, racing thoughts
- Boredom, seeking excitement
- Constant fidgeting
- Attention difficulties
- Impatience
- Professional/academic challenges
- Relationship complexities

- Health and financial issues
- Lack of attention to details
- Careless mistakes
- Distractibility
- Incomplete tasks
- Forgetfulness
- Task switching
- Impulsive actions
- Excessive talking
- Losing/forgetting items
- Oppositional Defiant Disorder (ODD)
- Depression
- Anxiety Disorders
- Bipolar Disorder
- Conduct Disorder
- Learning Disorder
- Substance Misuse
- Autism Spectrum Disorders

How many did you encircle, highlight or checkmark? Do you think you have ADHD at this point?

The Process of Getting an ADHD Diagnosis

Okay, so let's say you're pretty sure you have ADHD but want a definite diagnosis to be sure. What should you expect? Healthline.com beautifully summarizes what you can expect from the diagnosis process, and it is as follows:

- Talk to a doctor or psychologist about your medical history and current challenges.
- Be ready to discuss your childhood, including grades and behavior. Old report cards can be handy here.
- ADHD signs should have been there before age 12, so you'll chat about early symptoms.
- Focus on your current struggles, like work, relationships, and how you manage tasks.
- You may need to complete questionnaires on ADHD traits, and others close to you might contribute too.
- Expect additional tests to rule out learning disabilities or similar disorders.
- A medical check-up to exclude other causes for your symptoms.
- Get recommendations, search online, and meet different professionals to find the best fit for you (Srakocic, 2021).

These basic steps should give you a better idea of what to expect when going for a diagnosis, but what of your emotional journey? Well, many adults who received this diagnosis experienced a mixture of emotions. This rollercoaster, based on real-life experiences, includes the following:

- Relief
- Anger
- Grief
- Optimism
- Validation
- Acceptance

- Overwhelm
- Forgiveness
- Indignation.
- Hope

Each person's journey is unique, but these shared emotional experiences emphasize the profound impact of an ADHD diagnosis on self-awareness and self-acceptance (ADDitude Editors, 2022).

Living With ADHD

Coming to terms with ADHD as something that sticks around for life can be tough when you're an adult. At first, it might feel like a big challenge, and you could be worried about what it means for your future. But as time goes on, you might start seeing the positive side of things. ADHD isn't just a problem; it comes with its own set of strengths.

Shifting how you see it—from just a challenge to a part of who you are—can help you feel more positive about it. Accepting ADHD means recognizing both the tough parts and the good sides, finding ways to deal with the challenges, and making it a part of your journey of self-discovery and growth.

Take it From Someone Who Went Through It

You're definitely not alone in navigating ADHD; many adults experience similar journeys. My own path to accepting ADHD has been transformative. Initially, it was tough, but I came to see my heightened creativity and intense focus as strengths, embracing the unique positives of ADHD.

Reflecting on life before and after medication, the change is stark. Pre-medication, my emotions were chaotic; I hopped between relationships and friendships, and my hobbies, like quad riding, were dangerously impulsive. It felt like I was constantly searching for something, struggling to find my true self.

However, post-diagnosis and starting medication, my life took a positive turn. I grew more patient, particularly with my kids, and found stability in my relationships, thanks to a supportive partner who gets my ADHD journey. Medication brought control over my impulsiveness and risky behaviors, leading to fewer hospital visits and a safer lifestyle. It's been a journey of positive changes and better handling of life's challenges!

Common Emotions When Accepting ADHD As a Lifelong Condition

Although it turned out to be positive, it didn't necessarily make the lows any better. But if you know what common emotions to expect, it won't catch you off guard. So, here are some emotions I definitely felt and some you can expect as well:

- **Anger**: Before managing my ADHD, anger was a constant, uncontrollable force. Minor conflicts would blow up, and I'd struggle to let go, getting caught in cycles of tension and discord.

- **Sadness**: I also battled deep sadness and depression, which chipped away at my self-esteem. The weight of these emotions felt like a heavy shadow over everything, making it hard to see any positives.
- **Impulsiveness**: To cope, I'd often shop impulsively, which only led to debt and financial strain. It was a tough cycle to break, but with my husband's support, we managed to get back on track.
- **Relief**: The real turning point came with my ADHD diagnosis. Initially, it was overwhelming, but finding ways to manage it, like medication, yoga, and meditation, brought a sense of hope and control. It was about learning to live with ADHD, not trying to rid myself of it.

Realizing that ADHD can't be completely cured was tough, but learning about ways to ease its symptoms was a game-changer. Medication became a key part of managing ADHD, along with other cool strategies like music, yoga, meditation, and exercise. These methods together helped calm my mind and ease ADHD effects. Gradually, they led to a more balanced life, bringing hope and a feeling of control in dealing with ADHD's ups and downs.

Strategies to Cope With Your ADHD Diagnosis

Exercise, yoga, and meditation have been key for me in managing intense emotions. At first, I wasn't sure why they worked, but now I see how they channel my overactive imagination into something positive, helping process and release built-up feelings. These practices use that extra energy for emotional regulation in a constructive way.

Remember, what works for one person might not work for another, so it's worth exploring different strategies for handling tough emotions. Take Paula, who was diagnosed with ADHD at 31. She shared her story and strategies to help others navigate similar challenges. Her list of coping methods could offer some insights for you, too. She did the following:

1. **Learn About ADHD**: Get the real scoop on ADHD and break down those myths.
2. **Find Help**: Partner with a healthcare pro for treatments like meds or therapy.
3. **Understand Its Impact**: Reflect on how ADHD affects your daily life for better clarity.
4. **Feel Your Emotions**: Allow yourself to fully experience your feelings guilt-free.
5. **Acknowledge Your Strengths**: Celebrate your talents and the positive things you offer.
6. **Challenge Negative Thoughts**: Rethink those negative beliefs about your ADHD.
7. **Talk About It**: Share your experiences with trusted friends or family.
8. **Join the ADHD Community**: Connect with others who have ADHD online or in support groups (Paula, 2022).

Remember, this journey is unique to each individual. Trust your own process, take what is helpful, and leave what is not. You're on a path toward acceptance, and it's okay to take it at your own pace.

Building Emotional Muscle

Building emotional muscle essentially means having emotional resilience. It refers to the internal strength that allows you to adapt, bounce back, and navigate life's challenges with a positive mindset. For adults with ADHD, it plays a crucial role in facing the unique hurdles posed by the condition. It's knowing and understanding how to live with your ADHD; imagine it as the sturdy anchor that keeps you grounded amidst the storms of daily life.

But what if you don't have emotional resilience? Then, you might experience something called emotional dysregulation, which is crucial. Healthline explains that it manifests when individuals struggle to control their emotional responses, resulting in a rollercoaster experience for many adults with ADHD (Lovering, 2022).

Emotional dysregulation in adults with ADHD can manifest as the following:

- sudden and intense outbursts of anger over minor frustrations,
- periods of overwhelming sadness or frustration that seem disproportionate to the situation and

- Impulsive, emotional reactions that lead to regrettable decisions, like blurting out thoughts without considering the consequences.

Without strong emotional muscles, the dysregulation will only become worse. Of course, there are ways to build your emotional muscles, which Lovering summarizes as the following:

- **Label Emotions**: Start by recognizing and naming your feelings. It's the first step to understanding and handling them better.
- **Slowing Down**: When emotions hit fast, try to slow down. It gives you a moment to think and react more calmly.
- **Identify Physical Signs**: Notice how your body reacts to emotions. These signs can clue you into what you're feeling.
- **Mindfulness Practices**: Try mindfulness, like meditation or cognitive-behavioral therapy, to boost emotional control.
- **Lifestyle Harmony**: Keep a balanced lifestyle – get enough sleep, eat well, and exercise regularly to support emotional health.
- **Co-regulation for Parents**: For parents, be warm and supportive. Use co-regulation strategies to create a calming family environment (Lovering, 2022).

Building emotional muscle means recognizing and understanding your emotions, regulating reactions to setbacks, and maintaining a sense of balance. It's the key to surviving and thriving, allowing individuals to build a foundation of strength that positively influences various aspects of their personal and professional lives.

Activity: Reflecting on Your ADHD Journey

Now that you know the ins and outs of ADHD symptoms and diagnosis, take some time to do this activity. Grab a pen and paper or open a digital document, and let's explore your emotions.

1. Current Emotions: Write down the emotions you're currently experiencing about your ADHD journey or your health journey. Be honest and open with yourself.

2. Ask yourself these questions:

- What challenges are you currently facing in your ADHD journey or health journey?
- Are there specific achievements or progress that you're proud of?
- How do you feel about the support you receive from yourself or others?
- Are there aspects of your journey that bring you joy or satisfaction?
- Do you have any concerns or fears about the future of your health journey?

3. Deeper Reflection: Take a moment to reflect on the prompts. Consider why you feel a certain way and if there are underlying emotions or thoughts you may not have fully explored.

4. Future Intentions: Based on your reflections, jot down a few intentions or goals for your ADHD journey or health journey.

Remember, this activity is a personal exploration, and there are no right or wrong answers. It's an opportunity to connect with your emotions and gain insights into your journey. Take your time, and be kind to yourself throughout this process.

We've covered the diagnosis journey and laid the groundwork for boosting your emotional strength. Now, let's dive into what sparks those ADHD quirks. Chapter 3 is your toolkit for spotting the triggers and mastering the art of steering your mood and reactions.

Chapter 3

Identifying Triggers and Emotional Regulation

E ver felt like your emotions are riding a roller coaster, and you're just along for the journey? You're not alone. This chapter helps you grab the controls. You will dive into what sets off our ADHD quirks and explore strategies to navigate your flow of emotions. Consider this your practical guide for handling the day-to-day challenges of feelings and reactions.

This isn't just theory – it's a hands-on handbook for understanding the intricacies of your emotional landscape. Think of it as gaining access to your emotional control room. We're embarking on the detective work of identifying triggers and honing emotional regulation skills.

So, gear up for some eye-opening insights that will help you take charge of your emotional exploration. Together, armed with practical tools, we're turning those unpredictable emotional moments into a more controlled and enjoyable experience. So let's get started!

Understanding Your Triggers

Think about triggers as hidden buttons in your environment, relationships, or yourself. When you (or someone or something) press those buttons, it creates a chain reaction of emotional responses or ADHD symptoms. That means you experience a rollercoaster of symptoms and emotions whenever triggered.

Take Simone, for example, diligently working on a project with a looming deadline. Then, a colleague starts tapping their pen rhythmically. Simone becomes irritated, which only turns into frustration. Then, her focus wavers, and her impulsivity takes over. Simone comments on the noise, causing a chain reaction – heightened emotions, increased impulsivity, and a struggle to regain control.

Now, let's reimagine Simone's example as if she understands her triggers. The rhythmic pen tapping of a nearby colleague triggers a familiar irritation. However, armed with an understanding of personal triggers, Simone takes a deep breath, acknowledging the potential escalation. Instead of reacting impulsively, Simone calmly addresses the noise issue, leading to a more constructive conversation. By recognizing and understanding triggers, Simone effectively manages emotions. She also curbs impulsivity and maintains focus – turning a potential flare-up into a moment of self-awareness and control.

These types of situations are typical for adults with ADHD. And although pen tapping might not trigger you, there certainly are others. Let's have a look at some common triggers for someone with ADHD:

- **Emotional Situations:** Difficulty regulating emotions and intense reactions to emotional situations can make it challenging for individuals with ADHD to manage their behavior.
- **Dietary Factors:** Consuming heavily processed foods, certain dietary supplements, and being exposed to environmental toxins may worsen ADHD symptoms.
- **Environmental Factors:** Exposure to toxins, pesticides in food, and air pollution, particularly fine particulate matter, can affect executive functioning, attention, and emotion regulation.
- **Family Dynamics:** High levels of family conflict, especially among teenagers with ADHD, can contribute to the severity of symptoms.
- **Life Events and Stress:** Significant life events such as work conflicts, divorce, and financial insecurity can intensify ADHD symptoms in adults.
- **Trauma:** Physical punishment at a young age, bullying at school, and ongoing struggles with emotional dysregulation can worsen ADHD symptoms.

- **Social Anxiety:** Difficulties in social communication, including challenges in developing and maintaining friendships, can lead to anxiety, depression, and social isolation (Loos, 2023).

As you read through this, think about what triggers you. Do you resonate with the list above? Chances are that you can quickly name a few things that flare up your symptoms or create emotional responses. But how do you manage them? Well, it starts with tracking the symptoms. Keeping track of your specific triggers will help you learn more about your ADHD patterns and manage the symptoms. Here are a few ways you can go about it, each with its benefits explained:

- **Diary or Journal:** Writing down daily experiences, emotions, and activities allows for reflecting on your day. It helps you identify patterns and correlations between specific triggers and ADHD symptoms over time.
- **Mobile Apps:** Apps designed for mood tracking and symptom monitoring provide a convenient way to record your daily experiences. Many apps offer visualizations and reports, making it easier to spot trends and triggers.
- **Calendar Reminders:** Setting regular reminders on a digital or physical calendar prompts you to reflect on your day. It aids in recognizing potential triggers and understanding how your daily activities impact ADHD symptoms.

- **Symptom Tracking Sheets:** Using structured tracking sheets to record specific symptoms and potential triggers provides a systematic approach. It allows you to create a holistic overview of triggers and how they affect your ADHD.
- **Mindfulness and Meditation:** Incorporating mindfulness will help you to stay in the moment and observe your thoughts and feelings without them taking over. Mindfulness can enhance self-awareness, making identifying triggers in real-time easier.
- **Collaboration with a Therapist:** Discussing your experiences with a therapist provides professional guidance. Therapists can help you explore triggers, offering personalized strategies and coping mechanisms.
- **Wearable Devices:** Some smartwatches and fitness trackers include features for monitoring stress levels and sleep patterns. These insights can contribute to understanding how lifestyle factors influence ADHD symptoms.
- **Self-Reflection Worksheets:** Structured worksheets that prompt self-reflection on daily experiences and emotional responses guide you in recognizing triggers. They can be tailored to focus specifically on ADHD symptoms.
- **Medication Log:** For those on medication, maintaining a log of medication intake and its effects clarifies how medication influences symptom triggers. It facilitates communication with healthcare providers for adjustments if needed.

- **Regular Check-Ins:** Scheduling regular self-check-ins to reflect on the day or week helps maintain consistent tracking. It's a simple yet effective method for ongoing awareness.

Ultimately, the choice of tracking method depends on your preferences and lifestyle. Consistent tracking not only helps identify triggers but also empowers you to manage your ADHD symptoms proactively.

Clinical Psychologist Dr. Sharon Saline emphasizes the importance of self-awareness through symptom tracking in building emotional resilience (Saline, 2022). Understanding your mental processes, also known as self-awareness, can be a game-changer when it comes to managing ADHD. Think of it as having a personalized GPS for your thoughts and actions. This skill involves recognizing your thinking patterns and what triggers adverse reactions.

When you work on this skill, it helps you understand and keep track of yourself better. That's super important for people with ADHD because it can be challenging to manage time, plan things, and stay focused. It's like having a special pass to see how your brain works behind the scenes. With this self-awareness, you can fine-tune how you approach tasks and projects. But it's not just about looking back; it's also about using that knowledge to make smart decisions in the moment. It helps you be more resilient and handle cognitive challenges more smoothly. You get to take control and make choices that make you perform at your best. It's all about personal growth and becoming more self-reliant. Pretty cool, right?

Managing Mood Swings and Emotional Outbursts

Managing emotions is a bit tricky for folks with ADHD. Well, they're like fireworks—super intense. So, imagine mood swings as these sudden shifts catch everyone off guard. It doesn't take much, like a bad grade or a minor spill, to turn a good mood into a not-so-great one.

The intensity can be wild, and sometimes it lasts all day, or poof, it's gone in 10 minutes. Here's the kicker: they might not realize how their behavior affects others during these mood swings.

Afterward, though, they often feel a bit guilty about it. It's not intentional, but sometimes, they need support navigating these emotional rollercoasters.

Because these mood swings and emotional outbursts can be exhausting, it's a good idea to learn how to manage them. And you don't have to follow all the methods. As long as you try a few things and pinpoint what works for you, you'll already notice a difference in your emotional stability. So, without further ado, here are a few things you can do to navigate those mood swings:

- **Connect with an ADHD Specialist:** Seek treatment from a professional who understands ADHD inside out. Having an expert can make a difference, whether it's therapy or medication.
- **Mindfulness Tailored for You:** While traditional mindfulness exercises might not hit the mark, try

adapting them to suit your style. Opt for movement-based meditations or focus on mentally engaging activities like music to find your Zen.

- **Pinpoint Your Triggers:** Keep a journal to track what sets off your mood swings. Recognizing patterns in your moods can empower you to anticipate and manage them more effectively.
- **March to Your Own Beat:** Embrace your uniqueness. Instead of fitting into conventional molds, find your own strategies and timelines. It can alleviate stress and frustration.
- **Reframe, Don't Blame:** Instead of viewing your symptoms as failures, see them as part of your unique makeup. Be kind to yourself, acknowledging that mood swings are a part of the ADHD journey.
- **Educate with Care:** Establish boundaries and educate others about ADHD when necessary. Keep go-to resources handy to share when you feel the need. Remember, you don't have to be the educator all the time.
- **Craft Your Social Media Space:** Curate a supportive corner on social media where you can connect with people who understand. Don't hesitate to mute, block, or report negativity, creating a safe online space (Gupta, 2023).

Remember, mood swings are part of the ADHD package, but with the right strategies and support, you can navigate them more smoothly. If you or someone you know is dealing with ADHD-related mood swings, reaching out to a mental health professional with ADHD expertise can make a significant difference.

Practical Strategies for Emotional Regulation

Before we go into practical strategies for emotional regulation, I'd like to introduce Emma. She is a 28-year-old with ADHD and is at home preparing for a dinner party. Unexpected guests arrive early, catching her off guard. The sudden change in plans triggers heightened stress and anxiety. In her overwhelmed state, she becomes irritable, expressing frustration at her guests for the unplanned early arrival, creating tension in the room.

In a similar home scenario but now using emotional regulation techniques, Emma takes a moment to recognize her escalating stress. She steps into another room, allowing herself a few deep breaths to center and calm her mind. Instead of expressing frustration, she returns to the gathering with a smile, welcoming the guests warmly. By reframing the situation positively, she adapts to the change smoothly. Emma's emotional regulation turns a potentially stressful moment into an enjoyable and flexible evening, strengthening connections with her guests.

Because everyone differs, there are a few emotional regulation techniques you can try. Psychotherapist Dr. Caroline Norman highlights ten tips for emotional regulation for ADHD adults, which is:

1. Attend to Physical Needs:

- Ensure sufficient sleep, regular meals, exercise, and outdoor time.
- Consider findings that highlight the importance of physical well-being in supporting emotional regulation.

2. Prioritize Regular Self-Care:

- Plan relaxing activities daily to prevent stress accumulation.
- Incorporate personalized self-care routines based on individual preferences.

3. Stay Present with Mindfulness:

- Focus on the present moment during emotional overwhelm.
- Utilize grounding techniques like listing sensory experiences or splashing cold water on the face.

4. Recognize Early Warning Signs:

- Identify signs of feeling overwhelmed and proactively manage triggers.
- Journal observations of early warning signs over a few days for increased self-awareness.

5. Challenge Negative Thoughts:

- Gently question and challenge negative thoughts; explore alternative explanations.
- Recognize that thoughts are not necessarily facts, especially in the context of ADHD.

6. Name and Understand Emotions:

- Please pay attention to emotions, name them, and evaluate their impact on situations.
- Journal responses to questions about emotional identification and reactions.

7. Pause and Reflect:

- When overwhelmed, pause, name the emotion, and assess alignment with long-term goals.
- Seek input from others or imagine the response of a non-ADHD friend for perspective.

8. Acknowledge the Validity of Emotions:

- Understand that emotions are a natural part of being human.
- Use healthy techniques like communication or writing to express emotions.

9. Boost Self-Esteem:

- Set achievable challenges, celebrate accomplishments, and engage in enjoyable hobbies.
- Foster self-compassion and replace self-criticism with understanding.

10. Consider Professional Support:

- Explore medication options under the guidance of a qualified ADHD professional.
- Seek professional assistance from Online-Therapy.com for a personalized toolkit and ongoing support (Dr. Norman, 2022).

Incorporating Dr. Norman's tips into daily life can improve emotional regulation for individuals with ADHD. It gives you a holistic approach, emphasizing physical well-being, self-awareness, and professional support when needed. And even if they don't all work for you, find out which ones do. That way, you create a list of coping mechanisms in your arsenal in case you need to combat surging mood swings.

Understanding Emotional Intelligence and its Benefits for ADHD

As you well know, ADHD brings its unique set of challenges, like distractions, impulsivity, and a constant whirlwind of thoughts. It creates a blur of overwhelming emotions that sometimes feel too heavy to bear. So, you might think about what emotional intelligence (EI) has to do with it. Well, it is a game-changer in managing the emotional side of the journey.

Sussan, a Psychiatric Mental Health Nurse Practitioner (PMHNP), says emotional intelligence is about recognizing and navigating feelings (Nwogwugwu, 2022). Think about it: as someone with ADHD, you may grapple with recognizing emotions and self-control, so developing EI becomes a vital tool.

It is your guide to understanding how emotions play out in your daily life. It helps you make sense of those moments when frustration or distraction hits. By honing emotional awareness and regulation, individuals with ADHD can better navigate the ups and downs, fostering a more balanced and empowered emotional state. For example, it can include some of the following benefits in your life:

- Enhanced Self-Awareness
- Improved Self-Regulation
- Increased Empathy
- Better Interpersonal Relationships
- Effective Communication
- Stress Management

- Goal Achievement
- Adaptability
- Problem-Solving Skills
- Increased Confidence

Like any skill, it takes active effort to learn emotional intelligence. Luckily, there are things you can do to improve yours. Some EI enriching skills, as seen on a platform that specializes in EI, include the following:

- **Observe your feelings:** Set reminders to pause and identify emotions.
- **Behavior awareness:** Connect actions with emotions for better self-management.
- **Question opinions:** Challenge viewpoints to broaden your understanding.
- **Take responsibility:** Own your emotions and behaviors for a positive impact.
- **Celebrate and reflect:** Acknowledge positive moments and reflect on negatives.
- **Breathe and stay calm:** Use breathing techniques to manage stress and maintain composure.
- **Continuous improvement:** Actively work on your EI as a lifelong practice, just like ADHD is a lifelong companion.
- **Acknowledge triggers:** take time to notice what triggers your emotions so you can learn to adapt.
- **Channel energy productively:** Redirect negative emotions into motivation.

- **Scheduling for efficiency:** Stick to schedules to effectively complete tasks.
- **Healthy Eating:** Maintain a balanced diet for your emotional well-being.
- **Stay Interested:** Consciously engage in subjects for emotional balance.
- **Set Exciting Goals:** Define motivating goals based on your strengths.
- **Positive Mindset:** View setbacks as learning opportunities.
- **Lifelong Learning:** Keep curious about gaining new knowledge.
- **Comfort Zone Challenge:** Embrace discomfort for your personal growth.
- **Seek and Offer Help:** Don't hesitate to seek or provide assistance wherever necessary.
- **Active Listening:** Prioritize listening to others for better understanding.
- **Approachability:** Strive to remain approachable at work or home.
- **Perspective-Taking:** Try to understand others' viewpoints for better conflict resolution.
- **Openness Fosters Connections:** Share experiences with others for genuine connections.
- **Develop One Skill:** Focus on improving one social skill at a time.
- **Walk in Others' Shoes:** Practice empathy for improved social skills.
- **Consistent Practice:** Regularly practice social interactions for improvement.

- **Face-to-Face Engagement:** Take social interactions offline for meaningful connections.
- **Networking Opportunities:** Attend local events for social skill development.
- **Nonverbal Awareness:** Mindfully use nonverbal cues in communication.
- **Actively Engage:** Participate in social activities to apply learned skills (Martin, 2022).

This list can be overwhelming; you don't have to do everything. But, if you start with one action, it's an excellent way to begin your EI-boosting journey.

Activity: Identify Your Triggers and Emotional Responses

We're at that part of the chapter where you get to apply what you've learned. Don't worry; it's not like the tedious history homework you had to do at school. Instead, it's a fun way to get to know yourself better and learn to recognize and cope with your specific ADHD triggers.

Remember, a trigger is a stimulus that can lead to an emotional or behavioral response. And for someone with ADHD, it means their symptoms might become worse, more frequent, or more overwhelming.

Step 1: Describe the Problem.

When you experience a trigger, what specific challenge or issue arises? Clearly define the problem in the space below.

Example: Feeling overwhelmed and anxious when faced with a cluttered workspace

_____

_____

_____

_____

_____

Step 2: Describe Your Worst-Case Scenario:

Consider the worst possible outcome when the trigger is activated. What do you fear might happen? Please write it down below.

Example: Missing an important deadline due to difficulty focusing in a cluttered environment.

_____

_____

_____

_____

_____

Step 3: Categorize Your Triggers:

Categorize your triggers into different categories, as listed below:

Example: Cluttered Workspace → Sensory Stimuli

Emotional state:

_____

_____

_____

_____

People:

_____

_____

_____

_____

Places:

_____

_____

_____

_____

Things:

_____

_____

_____

_____

Thoughts:

_____

_____

_____

_____

Activities:

_____

_____

_____

_____

Sensory Stimuli:

_____

_____

_____

_____

Others (Specify):

_____

_____

_____

_____

Step 4: Identify Your Three Biggest Triggers:

Please list your top three triggers based on their impact on your emotional well-being.

    A. *Example:* Cluttered Workspace
    B. *Example:* Interrupted Routine
    C. *Example:* Unstructured Tasks

_____

_____

_____

_____

Step 5: Write Down Your Strategies to Reduce Exposure:

Identify ways to avoid or minimize exposure to each trigger. What actions can you take to lessen their impact?

Example: Organize and declutter your workspace regularly to maintain a clean environment.

_____

_____

_____

_____

_____

_____

Step 6: Consider How You Will Deal with Your Triggers:

Despite efforts to avoid triggers, they may still arise. Develop coping mechanisms for each trigger.

Example: Cluttered Workspace - Take short breaks to declutter and use visual aids for organization.

_____

_____

_____

_____

_____

_____

When you've completed this list, it should give you a better idea of your specific triggers. It also allows you to think about avoidance or coping strategies in an untriggered state. That way, you can proactively manage your emotional responses, boost your emotional intelligence, and navigate challenges effectively.

As you get better at handling your triggers and emotions, you'll start to see the unique strengths that come with having ADHD. In the next chapter, we'll explore these 'ADHD Superpowers' and learn how to use them to your advantage.

Chapter 4

Embracing Your Unique ADHD Superpowers

"Everybody is a genius. But if you judge a fish by its ability to climb a tree, it will live its whole life believing that it is stupid."

— *Albert Einstein*

This quote made me chuckle, but I also felt more understood. As an adult with ADHD, it's become the norm to be judged according to neurotypical standards. And what did that create? I spent a whole childhood thinking that there was something wrong with me, feeling guilty, and all the other emotions that come with that journey.

But now that I've got the diagnosis and learned to embrace its unique superpowers, I feel more like myself than ever before. That's what this chapter is all about. It will show you that ADHD is not just a set of problems but also comes with its own unique strengths. And when you discover and harness these so-called "superpowers," you will have a more fulfilling life.

The Unique Strengths of ADHD

Let's talk about the fantastic side of ADHD that often gets overshadowed. It is things you might not have thought about as strengths. Think back for a moment: did you notice increased levels of creativity, focus, and resilience? If so, guess what: not everyone experiences them. People with ADHD often bring a truckload of creativity to the table.

Ever find yourself thinking outside the box, coming up with ideas that make heads turn? That's the ADHD spark right there. Or have you ever started a project and suddenly lost track of time because you were so deeply engrossed? That's your hyperfocus at play—a superpower that can turn ordinary tasks into extraordinary feats. And what about resilience? How many times did you try and fail at something without feeling defeated? Chances are that you've gotten up after defeat more than you can count. That's your resilient nature, thanks to ADHD.

The thing about these traits is that they might not fit the traditional mold of "normal." But not being "normal" under a neurotypical lens means you're just a fish that's being judged for not being able to climb. And it is when you recognize these strengths, you unlock a treasure chest within yourself. It changes the whole perspective on ADHD. It's not just about challenges; it's about a set of remarkable abilities that make you stand out in a crowd. Numerous studies highlight the positive side of ADHD, focusing on real stories rather than just numbers.

In a 2006 study, people with and without ADHD were asked to draw animals for a different planet and create a new toy. Unsurprisingly, people with ADHD showed extra creativity compared to those without the condition (Nall, 2021). Another study in 2017 on adults with ADHD explored creativity by having them think of new uses for everyday items (Nall, 2021).

Surprisingly, those with and without ADHD had a similar number of ideas, regardless of medication. However, when there was a chance to win a bonus, those with ADHD generated more ideas, suggesting rewards could motivate them. In essence, these studies support the idea that people with ADHD often possess creativity and innovation.

At the same time, personal accounts consistently highlight the energetic, creative, courageous, and resilient nature of individuals with ADHD. This positive perspective, backed by the potential benefits of ADHD medication, paves the way for a more positive and balanced life with ADHD (Burch, 2022).

Real-life Stories of ADHD Superpowers

If you're still thinking that this ADHD superpower thing isn't real, think again. Many people have the diagnosis and decide to use it, including some celebrities; of course, ADDitude gives us a few examples of celebrities with ADHD who thrive despite and because of their diagnosis (ADDitude Editors, 2016).

Simone Biles is an incredible gymnastics prodigy who fearlessly embraced her ADHD, showing the world that it's okay to seek treatment and normalize it Her triumphs in the gymnastic world are a testament to her thriving with ADHD.

Shane Victorino, a professional MLB player, faced childhood challenges and hyperactive tendencies that highlighted the importance of early ADHD diagnosis. His story underscores the significance of managing ADHD symptoms, allowing him to thrive on the baseball field.

Emma Watson, known for her roles in Hogwarts and as a UN ambassador, has had an ADHD journey filled with academic success and impactful roles. Medication for ADHD became a supportive ally, empowering Watson to navigate both academia and the global stage.

Jon Favreau, a director, had a revelation about his ADHD during the creation of "Everything Everywhere All at Once," shedding light on his creative process. This newfound understanding became a catalyst for self-discovery, marking a pivotal moment in Favreau's artistic exploration.

Trevor Noah, a comedian, openly discusses the link between his ADHD and depression, revealing the complex relationship between mental health conditions. Noah's journey emphasizes the importance of holistic self-care, acknowledging the intricate interplay of ADHD and depression.

Adam Levine, who you might know as Maroon 5's lead singer, found his ADHD therapy in music, offering him a sense of control amidst mental chaos. Levine's openness encourages others to find constructive outlets, showcasing that ADHD can coexist with success in the music industry.

Lisa Ling, a journalist, experienced relief and clarity after revealing her adult ADHD diagnosis. Ling's story echoes the transformative power of self-awareness, inspiring those with ADHD to seek understanding and acceptance.

Raven Baxter, a molecular biologist known as Dr. Raven the Science Maven, champions ADHD visibility. By sharing her ups and downs, Baxter demonstrates the potential for success when embracing one's ADHD journey in the realm of science communication.

Dave Grohl, the frontman of Foo Fighters, candidly admits to his ADHD and academic struggles, highlighting the liberating effect of self-acceptance. Grohl's journey from a disengaged student to an iconic musician reflects the transformative power of embracing ADHD as an integral part of one's identity.

Mel Robbins, an author and speaker, received a late ADHD diagnosis but didn't let it deter her from candidly addressing its impact on her life. Robbins' story is a testament to resilience, urging individuals with ADHD to navigate challenges while embracing their unique strengths.

These remarkable individuals not only identified their ADHD but also harnessed its strengths to excel in their respective fields. Their stories encourage embracing neurodiversity, challenging stereotypes, and celebrating the unique perspectives ADHD brings to their extraordinary journeys.

Tips to Harness Your ADHD Strengths

At this point, how did you perceive your symptoms? Did it feel like a burden or weakness, Or did you feel proud of your abilities? If it's the first, know that you aren't alone in what you're feeling. But, you have the ability to reshape your mindset about them. And the best way to do that is to learn how to identify, develop, and apply them to your daily life.

When you have ADHD, you can improve your chances for success, according to your standards, by focusing on your natural talents (Giwerc, n.d.) David Giwerc is the founder of the ADD Coach Academy and emphasizes the importance of identifying your ADHD strengths to improve your life. He suggests the following ways to explore your strengths and make them stronger:

1. Discover Your Strengths: Identify what truly captures your attention. To develop this, consciously notice activities that make you lose track of time or absorb you completely. In your life, this skill means you can channel your focus into tasks you're genuinely interested in, leading to increased productivity and a sense of accomplishment.

2. Dive into Enjoyable Tasks: Identify tasks that bring joy and that satisfying feeling of "I can handle this." To develop this, make a list of activities that consistently bring you happiness. Integrating these tasks into your routine can make daily life more enjoyable, reduce stress, and boost overall well-being.

3. Navigate Away from Boredom: Steer clear of tasks that trigger boredom and disinterest. To develop this, recognize when you start feeling bored or disinterested and find ways to make those tasks more engaging, such as turning them into a game or setting a time limit. This skill allows you to avoid procrastination and complete tasks more efficiently.

4. Understand Your Interest Triggers: Unpack why specific tasks are interesting to you. To develop this, reflect on what aspects of certain activities captivate your attention. This understanding helps you intentionally choose tasks that align with your interests, leading to increased motivation and engagement.

5. Break Down Your Winning Strategies: Deconstruct how you naturally approach a task. To develop this, analyze the steps you take when successfully completing a task and create a quick guide or checklist. This can enhance your organizational skills, making it easier to tackle complex projects.

6. Set Up Visual or Auditory Reminders: Craft a visual map or a speedy audio track as reminders of your winning formula. To develop this, use visual aids or recorded reminders to reinforce the steps that contribute to your success. This practice supports consistency and helps you stay on track.

7. Apply Your Success Moves Everywhere: Take your winning strategies to new territories. To develop this, consciously apply the successful approaches you've identified in one area to other aspects of your life.

This versatility transforms your strengths into a universal toolkit, empowering you to overcome challenges across various domains.

Harnessing your ADHD strengths is a game-changer. Think about work: your creativity kicks in, making problem-solving a breeze. Hyperfocus: It turns projects into top-notch achievements. In relationships, your open communication about expectations leaves little space for misinterpretation. On top of that, your spontaneous playfulness makes for fun relationship magic, And that resilience you've built up over the years It's your superhero ability to bounce back from anything. These strengths aren't just for show; they're the key to turning your daily challenges into success stories, one relationship and project at a time.

ADHD and Creativity

ADHD and creativity go hand-in-hand, and chances are that you've experienced it before. You know those times when your mind just fires off ideas left and right? Well, that's the ADHD creativity taking center stage. It lets you think outside the box, take risks, and come up with new ideas on the fly.

Understanding the connection between ADHD and creativity is really fascinating. While there isn't concrete evidence, it seems that certain traits of ADHD actually help boost creative thinking. Take impulsivity, for example. It's interesting because it can spark original ideas by quieting that inner critic we all have. And even though distraction can be a challenge, we can also see it as an asset because it brings together different elements in the mind and leads to fresh concepts.

In academic settings, people with ADHD often excel at generating new ideas, while people without ADHD tend to focus more on existing ones (Kelly, n.d.) The arts are a great example of this, with well-known figures like Will.i.am and Alejandro González Iñárritu, who have ADHD and have achieved great success. But please remember that having ADHD doesn't automatically mean you have artistic talent. Instead, it means that traits like taking risks and having an intense focus on personal interests can definitely contribute to creative growth.

Of course, ADHD does come with its own set of challenges, especially when it comes to planning, time management, and completing tasks. However, by recognizing creativity as a strength and working on organizational skills, you can overcome these challenges and allow your creative potential to truly thrive.

If you're looking to "unlock your creative potential," The ADHD Center has a few tips you can follow to do just that:

1. **Own your awesome ADHD brain:** It might not be neurotypical, but it amazingly sees the world through a different lens.
2. **Spot what triggers intense focus**: where your hyper-focusing goes, creativity flourishes.
3. **Try tools to organize your creative chaos:** try mind-mapping, brainstorming, or even journaling.

4. **Jot down ideas on the fly:** you never know when unexpected inspiration will strike.

5. **Team up with others:** when someone else has skills complementary to yours, it might help boost your organization, focus, and creativity.

6. **Cheer for your creative wins:** celebrate even the smallest victories!

7. **Dare to take risks and learn from mistakes:** you might just have a creative breakthrough after experiencing failure.

8. **Manage your focus:** try meditation or noise-cancelling headphones to decrease distractions (The ADHD Centre, 2023).

By following these tips, you'll boost productivity and embrace creativity as a super-strength. It will help enhance your efficiency and tap into your ADHD's creative potential. At the same time, it lets you navigate tasks with ingenuity. And you don't necessarily have to use these steps just to hone your creativity. You can also use them in various aspects of your life to make living with your ADHD a breeze.

Activity: Understanding Your ADHD Strengths

This activity will help you to understand your unique ADHD strengths and how to harness them. Take some time to follow the instructions below, and who knows, You might just learn something new about yourself today.

1. Identify Your Interests:

- List activities or tasks that consistently captivate your interest and bring you joy.
- Reflect on why these activities are interesting to you.

2. Focus on Enjoyable Tasks:

- Identify tasks, goals, or projects that you find enjoyable and fulfilling.
- Consider how these tasks make you feel and why you find them satisfying.

3. Navigate Boredom and Disinterest:

- Acknowledge instances where ADHD challenges manifest as boredom or disinterest.
- Think about strategies to make these tasks more engaging or exciting.

4. Reflect on Interest Triggers:

- Explore specific factors that make certain topics, goals, or tasks interesting to you.
- Consider how understanding these triggers can enhance your engagement.

5. Identify Success Steps:

- Reflect on the steps you naturally take when focusing on a subject that leads to task completion.
- Create a list of these success steps.

6. Create Visual or Auditory Reminders:

- Transform your list of success steps into a visual map or an audio recording.
- Explore how these reminders can reinforce the steps contributing to your success.

7. Apply Success Strategies Across Areas:

- Consider how the strategies that enable success in one area can be applied to overcome challenges in other areas.
- Identify specific areas where you can implement these strategies.

8. Uncover Clues to Organizing Your Life:

- Reflect on how identifying your strengths and interests unveils clues to creating a system for organizing your life.
- Consider how this system can promote sustained focus and consistent action.

9. Reflection Time:

Now that you have all your answers, take a few minutes to reflect on the questions below.

- What surprised you the most about your strengths and interests?
- How can you leverage your strengths in different aspects of your life, such as work or relationships?
- Are there additional strengths you've discovered through these self-assessments? If yes, what are they?

Remember, this self-assessment is a starting point for recognizing and harnessing your unique strengths associated with ADH. It's a journey of self-discovery and empowerment.

Having explored the unique strengths that come with ADHD, it's time to channel these "superpowers" into your daily life. In Chapter 5, we'll guide you through effective goal-setting strategies tailored for individuals with ADHD. Discover how to harness your strengths and navigate challenges as we delve into practical approaches to make your goals a reality.

Chapter 5

Goal-Setting for Success

I magine setting a goal and actually reaching it. That sounds impossible with ADHD, right? Wrong. The secret isn't in the goal itself but in how you approach it. As someone living with ADHD, traditional goal-setting rules don't apply to you, and that's okay. In this chapter, we explore tailored strategies that have been proven to work specifically for people with ADHD, guiding you through setting and achieving goals that make a real difference in your life.

Why Goal-Setting Matters with ADHD

Goal-setting is crucial in managing ADHD, acting as a roadmap for navigating the challenges. It's especially important because it offers a structured approach tailored to the unique workings of the ADHD brain. This structure can significantly ease ADHD symptoms. Take Chris, for example, a lively guy with ADHD. He faces a chaotic day filled with various tasks but lacks a clear plan. Without set goals, his ADHD symptoms intensify, and the clutter and looming deadlines only add to his anxiety and inability to focus.

In a situation like Chris's, the absence of goals makes the day overwhelming and disorganized. However, having clear, achievable goals could change the game. It would sharpen his focus, provide much-needed structure, reduce the sense of being overwhelmed, and enhance his motivation, turning a potentially stressful day into a more manageable and productive one.

- **Harnessing Focus with ADHD**: Clear goals help direct your energy and attention, acting like blinders to distractions. They keep you focused on what matters.
- **Adding Structure**: For ADHD minds, structure is key. Goals build this structure, bringing order to the often chaotic ADHD experience. Knowing your aims makes it easier to sort your thoughts and actions.
- **Tackling Overwhelm**: Goals break down overwhelming tasks into smaller, more manageable steps. It shifts your view from a daunting mountain to achievable steps, making tasks less intimidating.
- **Boosting Motivation**: Goals set a clear target, providing a tangible reward for your efforts. This is especially motivating for ADHD individuals, turning everyday tasks into steps towards bigger achievements. This sense of progress can be a strong motivator.

Setting goals can really help with ADHD symptoms. It adds structure and focus, tackling issues like memory troubles and attention difficulties. By making goals achievable and breaking them down into smaller steps, you can boost your well-being. ADHD-friendly tactics like splitting tasks into chunks, boosting self-motivation, managing your mood, and adopting healthy habits can help you deal with those challenges and succeed in various aspects of life.

How to Set Goals That Stick

You might be familiar with the SMART criteria for effective goal setting. And if you're not, don't worry; I'm about to fill you in. You see, this framework is a practical guide that helps you set clear goals from the get-go. In doing so, your goals won't be just another note on a forgotten piece of paper. Instead, it will stick and become achievable. But what does SMART stand for, you may ask? Let's unpack it:

S-Specific: Your goal needs to be crystal clear. Instead of saying, "get fit," try "go for a 30-minute walk every morning."

M-Measurable: Make sure you can track your progress. Instead of a vague "read more," aim for "finish one book every month."

A-Achievable: Dream big, but keep it real. Set goals that push you but are doable. Going from zero to running a marathon might be a stretch, but starting with a 5k is achievable.

R-Relevant: Your goal should matter to you. If it doesn't align with your values or needs, it's likely to fizzle out. If you hate running, don't make it a running goal.

T-Time-bound: Set a deadline. Without one, your goal is a bit like a ship without a captain. It needs direction and an endpoint. Instead of "learn a new language," try "spend 15 minutes daily learning Spanish for the next three months."

See, SMART isn't just a fancy concept; it's your ticket to turning goals from wishful thinking into tangible achievements. But the trick lies in being as specific as possible. There should be no room for interpretation when you revisit your goals later on. Setting personalized goals is a vital part of managing your ADHD and getting things done. Here are a few examples of vague vs. clear SMART goals:

1. Vague Goal: "Improve time management."

Specific Goal: "Reduce procrastination by using a time-blocking technique to allocate specific time slots for daily tasks. Complete a time audit at the end of each week to track progress."

2. Vague Goal: "Enhance communication skills."

Specific Goal: "Participate in a communication workshop to develop active listening skills. Practice summarizing key points in conversations and seek feedback from peers to improve clarity."

3. Vague Goal: "Achieve better work-life balance."

Specific Goal: "Establish a daily routine that includes dedicated work hours and designated personal time. Use a productivity app to track time spent on work tasks and leisure activities, aiming for a balanced distribution."

> *"When you write down your goals, you clarify your future. If you're not clear about what you want or where you want to go, you'll lack direction"*
>
> — *Pettit, 2020*

Of course, some goals might feel like a mountain in front of you, which can seem overwhelming. But, if you break them down into smaller short-term milestones, it could be less overwhelming and more manageable. Here are some steps you can take to do that:

1. Start by clearly defining your overarching goal, ensuring it meets the SMART criteria—specific, measurable, achievable, relevant, and time-bound.
2. Recognize the major steps or phases required to achieve your goal. These milestones signify substantial progress toward your ultimate objective.
3. Divide each milestone into smaller, more manageable goals. Think of it as tasks or objectives that can be accomplished within shorter time frames, like a week or a month.

4. For each sub-goal, outline the specific tasks that need completion. These are the daily or weekly actions you'll undertake to make progress.

5. Prioritize tasks based on their impact on achieving sub-goals and organize them logically. Develop a timeline or schedule to keep track of when each task should be completed.

6. Regularly review and monitor your progress. Acknowledge and celebrate small victories along the way to maintain motivation and momentum (Everyday Design, n.d.).

If your goals seem overwhelming, make them smaller. Remember, your goals shouldn't overwhelm you. Instead, they should motivate you to live the best life possible. And while it can be daunting at times, take it one small step at a time. Smaller victories make for bigger long-term success in whatever you wish to achieve.

Real-world Success Stories

Susan Baroncini-Moe and Brian Scudamore are real-world success stories when it comes to goal-setting. Both of them employed unique strategies that showcased the power of personalized goals (Bailey, 2017). Let's start with Susan. As an entrepreneur with ADHD, she embraced her diagnosis as an opportunity for growth. An ADHD coach became the core of her strategy. This coach not only held her accountable but also understood the specific challenges she faced. By creating personalized systems, staying organized, incorporating exercise and meditation, and scheduling tasks based on optimal functionality, Susan turned goal-setting into a transformative tool. Her positive changes include enhanced productivity, improved focus, and a continuous quest for self-optimization.

Then, we have Brian Scudamore, the CEO of O2E Brands. He harnessed the power of goal-setting by understanding his strengths and weaknesses. Adopting a "two-in-the-box" strategy allowed him to focus on his visionary strengths while his COO translated these visions into tangible business realities. Brian's tools and tricks, such as changing work locations to increase concentration, exemplify his commitment to efficiency. Through these strategies, he has not only managed his ADHD symptoms but leveraged them for success. Positive changes in Brian's life include streamlined business operations, improved focus, and a clear understanding of how to channel his energy effectively.

These stories illustrate that goal-setting when personalized and coupled with strategic approaches, not only addresses the challenges of ADHD but becomes a catalyst for positive and transformative changes.

Tools and Techniques for Achieving Your Goals

At this point, you know why goal setting is important and how to set goals that stick. Easy, right? Maybe for someone who is neurotypical, but my fellow ADHDers may need a little more help. That's where tools and techniques can help you achieve those beautifully crafted goals of yours. Zapier and Clickup share various apps or planners you can use to help your neuro-divergent mind with goal-tracking:

- **Amazing Marvin** is a highly customizable to-do list app with ADHD-friendly features like habit tracking and rewarding tasks.
- **TickTick** helps you focus on tasks with features like making lists, tasks, and tags. It also gives fun rewards when you tick something off your list.
- **Sunsama** is a really good time management app without too much complexity. You add your estimated completion time for a task, and the app helps you create a realistic plan for your day (Irish, 2023).
- **ClickUp** has more project management features. That means you can manage tasks and goals in a more structured way for the whole family.
- **Inflow** focuses on behavioral therapy, helping people with ADHD understand and manage their symptoms.
- **EndeavorRx,** approved by the FDA, is an ADHD video treatment app. While it is catered to children, adults can also benefit from it.
- **Routinery** helps you schedule your day while giving you rewards for your achievements. It includes audio reminders and visual timers for those who are neurodivergent.
- **AutoSilent** mutes your phone during scheduled times, allowing you to focus more on the tasks at hand instead of getting distracted.
- **SimpleMind Pro** provides a visually appealing way to structure your thoughts and planning process.

- **Dwellingright** allows you to categorize and manage your tasks. It also includes Artificial Intelligence (AI) suggestions and allows you to connect with your family members.
- **Brain Focus** is another time management app that allows you to categorize your tasks, disable distractions, and focus on priority activities.
- **Clear To-dos,** a clutter-free to-do list, is a minimalist app that helps you maintain focus on your daily tasks and goals.
- **Productive-Habit Tracker** helps you to build positive habits. It monitors your progress and has competition options to help instill lasting positive routines in your day (York, 2023).

As you can see, there are many different apps you can download to help achieve your goals. Although it can seem overwhelming, know you don't have to download them all. Try those that resonated with you the most and see if it works for you. If it does, great! Keep going. And if it doesn't, don't feel discouraged; try another one until you find what works for you.

Activity: Breaking Down Goals

Let's turn those big dreams into achievable wins! Take a moment to write down one significant long-term goal you want to achieve. Now, let's break it down into smaller, manageable steps using the SMART criteria: Specific, Measurable, Achievable, Relevant, and Time-bound. Use the format below to break down your goals and make them less daunting.

Example and Explanation:

Long-Term Goal: [Your Goal]

1. **Specific:** What do you want to accomplish, exactly? Be crystal clear.
2. **Measurable:** How will you measure or track your progress and know when you've reached each step?
3. **Achievable:** Are these steps realistic and attainable for you?
4. **Relevant:** Do these smaller goals align with your long-term vision?
5. **Time-bound:** Set a realistic timeline for each step.

Your Personal Goal Breakdown:

1. SMART Goal 1:

Specific:

_____

Measurable:

_____

Achievable:

_____

Relevant:

_____

Time-bound:

_____

2. SMART Goal 2:

Specific:

_____

Measurable:

_____

Achievable:

_____

Relevant:

_____

Time-bound:

_____

3. SMART Goal 3:

Specific:

_____

Measurable:

_____

Achievable:

_____

Relevant:

_____

Time-bound:

_____

4. SMART Goal 4:

Specific:

_____

Measurable:

_____

Achievable:

_____

Relevant:

_____

Time-bound:

_____

5. SMART Goal 5:

Specific:

Measurable:

Achievable:

Relevant:

Time-bound:

Feel free to use this template to guide your goal-setting journey. Breaking down your goals into smaller, SMART steps makes the path to success much more manageable and enjoyable!

Achieving your goals takes more than just setting them. In the next chapter, we'll explore how your lifestyle choices, like diet, exercise, sleep, and stress management, can be game changers.

Chapter 6

Lifestyle Changes

I n a world where the quest for improved focus and attention often leads to pharmaceutical solutions, there exists a wealth of lifestyle changes that can significantly impact the management of ADHD. Have you ever considered that a mere 20 minutes of exercise has the power to enhance your attention span for up to an hour (Vozza, 2015)? Or that the foods you choose can either support or hinder your journey in managing ADHD symptoms?

If you're tired of relying only on pills and want to explore other options, get ready for a big change. In the following pages, we'll go into the details of your daily routines - from your diet to your exercise, sleep, and stress management. You'll uncover the hidden secrets in your habits and learn how these seemingly ordinary aspects can become powerful tools for managing ADHD.

In this chapter, we will explore how lifestyle changes can go beyond medication for managing ADHD. We will discuss the relationships between exercise, nutrition, sleep, and stress management, empowering you to take control of your ADHD through your daily habits. From practical tips on incorporating exercise into your routine to understanding the impact of certain foods on cognitive function, each section of this chapter provides actionable knowledge.

The Food-Mood Connection

Picture this: You grab a quick, sugary snack during a hectic workday, and suddenly, it feels like your focus has hit a speed bump. Conversations blur, and tasks tangle up. Now, imagine the flip side—a day when you opt for a balanced meal, and clarity becomes your companion. That's the food-mood connection that those with ADHD are particularly sensitive to.

Paying attention to what you eat is important for more than just your food choices. It plays a big role in how your mood is connected to what you eat. If you have ADHD, understanding this connection can help you manage your symptoms better. Some foods can make ADHD symptoms worse or better, so choosing the right foods is important for your overall well-being.

Your diet can affect ADHD management in different ways. For example, taking amino acid supplements can affect the chemicals in your brain, and omega-3 fatty acids might also have an effect (Roybal, 2008). Trying elimination diets that focus on specific ingredients like additives or sugar can help you figure out which foods work best for you.

Managing ADHD is about more than just understanding your mind. It's also about knowing how the food you eat affects your emotions and ability to focus. For example, some foods can alleviate your symptoms while others can worsen it. Here's a list of foods to include and avoid in your daily diet, according to Medical News Today (Leonard, 2019):

Foods that may help alleviate ADHD symptoms:

1. **Fruits and Vegetables:** Research suggests that increased consumption of fruits and vegetables may improve symptoms of inattention associated with ADHD. Aim for about 2 cups of fruits and 2 cups of vegetables per day.

2. **Complex Carbohydrates:** Complex Carbohydrates: Go for fruits like berries and apples, whole grains like oatmeal or whole-wheat bread or pasta, and legumes like peas, beans, and lentils.

3. **Protein-rich Foods:** Include eggs, lean meat, milk, cheese, nuts, soy, and low-fat yogurt. Protein-rich breakfasts have been associated with enhanced mood, attention, and alertness.

4. **Healthy Fats:** Found in fatty fish, soybeans, walnuts, flaxseeds, tofu, chia seeds, and avocados, these fats may support heart health, memory, and immune function. Some studies suggest they could improve hyperactivity, impulsivity, and attention symptoms in ADHD.

Foods to limit or avoid with ADHD:

1. **Sugary Foods:** While the link between sugar consumption and ADHD symptoms is debated, it's generally advisable to limit high-sugar foods to promote overall health.
2. **Simple Carbohydrates:** Reduce intake of high-sugar foods, such as soda, candies, sweets, cakes, cookies, fruit juice concentrate, and processed foods like granola bars and potato chips.
3. **Unhealthy Fats:** A diet high in unhealthy saturated fats may be associated with symptoms of inattention in ADHD. Avoid fried foods, processed meat, butter, high-fat dairy products, and heavy cream.
4. **Caffeine:** Caffeine's impact on ADHD varies among individuals. Some may need to limit consumption due to potential side effects like insomnia, nervousness, irritability, stomach discomfort, and anxiety, especially if taking stimulant medications.

How many of these foods or drinks do you consume daily? And how many of them are on which list? If you're leaning more toward consuming ADHD-triggering foods, it's a good idea to adjust your diet. But it's not always as easy to do, is it?

Tips to Incorporate Beneficial Foods Into Your Diet

If you know you're supposed to eat healthier but don't know where to start, don't worry! Healthy diets aren't always on a neurodivergent's priority list. Luckily, there are a few things you can do to make your diet more nutritious, one step at a time, as approved by a dietician:

1. **Balanced Meals**: Mix grains, proteins, and fruits or veggies on your plate. This combo keeps your body healthy and your mind focused.
2. **Omega-3s for Your Brain**: Find them in fish, flax seeds, walnuts, and canola oil. Great for learning and behavior, especially with ADHD.
3. **Limit Sugary Stuff**: Cut down on candy and sweet snacks. They mess with your energy levels, which is not great for ADHD.
4. **Eat Regularly**: Have meals every few hours. Use phone alarms as reminders to keep your energy stable.
5. **Snack Smart**: Go for snacks that mix grains and protein, like cheese and crackers or yogurt with fruit. Tasty and energy-boosting!
6. **Visible Snacks**: Keep snacks where you can see them, like at your desk, so you don't forget to eat.
7. **Organize Your Kitchen**: Keep similar items together and label things in your fridge. It makes cooking and finding stuff easier.

8. **Grocery List**: Keep a list of staples and add to it weekly. This saves time and helps you remember everything.

9. **Prep Meals in Advance**: Cut veggies and cook food for the week. Ready-to-go meals are a lifesaver when you're busy.

10. **Use Pre-prepped Food**: It's okay to use pre-chopped or cooked foods or try meal delivery services for easy cooking.

Remember, these tips are here to help make eating easier and healthier for you, especially if you have ADHD. Keep it simple and fun!

Exercise Your Way to Stability

Have you ever noticed how good you feel after running around, playing a sport, or even just taking a brisk walk? That's because when we move our bodies, it's like giving our brain a super fun, happy boost! Exercise can really help in keeping your mood steady and bright, especially when you have ADHD.

When you exercise, your body releases cool stuff called endorphins. Think of them as tiny little cheerleaders in your body, making you feel happy and calm. Plus, exercise helps use up extra energy, which can be super helpful if you find yourself feeling fidgety or restless a lot.

Now, not all exercise has to be the same, and the best part is you can pick what works for you! Here are some awesome types of exercises that are great for people with ADHD:

1. **Running or Jogging**: This is a super easy way to get started. Running helps clear your mind and gives you a sense of freedom.
2. **Team Sports**: Sports like soccer, basketball, or baseball are not only fun, but they also help you learn to work as part of a team. Plus, they're a great way to make friends!
3. **Martial Arts**: This is really cool because it teaches you about focus, discipline, and control. Plus, you get to learn some awesome moves!
4. **Swimming**: If you love being in the water, swimming can be a great way to exercise. It's also really relaxing and helps you feel at peace.
5. **Yoga**: Yoga is all about balance and calming your mind. It's a great way to stretch out your muscles and learn how to breathe deeply, which can help a lot when you're feeling stressed.
6. **Dance**: Turn on your favorite music and dance around! It's a fun way to exercise and express yourself at the same time. You can even join a dance class if you want to learn some new moves.
7. **Biking**: Riding a bike is not just a way to get around; it's also a fantastic way to exercise. It allows you to explore new places and enjoy some fresh air while you're at it.

8. **Hiking or Nature Walks**: Walking in nature is a great way to get exercise, and it's super calming, too. You get to explore, see cool plants and animals, and breathe in the fresh air.

Remember, the best exercise is the one you enjoy because that's the one you'll keep doing. So, find something fun and stick with it. You'll be surprised how much it can help in keeping your mood stable and making you feel great!

How Exercise Maintains Focus and Reduces Impulsivity

Apart from stabilizing your mood, exercise is also a good way to help you stay focused and less impulsive. Did you know that moving around and playing can make your brain sharper? A study by Dr. Betsy Hoza found that just 30 minutes of fun exercise every day can make kids with ADHD focus better and feel happier (Miller, 2016).

When you exercise, your body makes special stuff like dopamine that helps you pay better attention. It's like a super-power for your brain that makes you more alert and ready to learn. At the same time, it helps you control your actions better, so you don't do things too quickly without thinking. It's like having a superhero in your body that helps you stay calm and make better choices. And guess what? Exercising outside is even better! When you play or exercise in nature, it helps calm your brain even more and makes it easier to manage ADHD symptoms (Special Strong, 2023).

Practical Tips on Making Exercise a Routine

Okay, so you know it's good for your ADHD to exercise. But because of your ADHD, you might find it difficult to make it a habit. A typical ADHD scenario is that you might hyperfocus on it for a few days or weeks, then move on to something else. If you relate, don't worry! Here are a few tips you can use to make exercise part of your daily routine:

1. **Pick Fun Activities**: Choose exercises you love. It's way more fun that way.
2. **Short and Sweet**: Do short bursts of exercise. Even 10 minutes here and there is awesome.
3. **Set Reminders**: Use your phone to remind you when it's time to move.
4. **Workout Buddy**: Exercise with friends. It's more fun and keeps you going.
5. **Try Yoga**: It's great for calming your mind and keeping fit (Illiades, 2013).
6. **Reward Yourself**: Treat yourself after working out. It's a great motivator.
7. **Just Right for You**: Do what feels good for you, not what you think you should do.
8. **Plan It**: Schedule your exercise like any important appointment.
9. **Prepare Ahead**: Get your workout gear ready beforehand to avoid excuses.
10. **Tell Someone**: Share your exercise plans with a friend or family for extra motivation.

11. **Every Bit Counts**: Remember, a little exercise is still good. Start small and build up.
12. **Be Positive**: Be kind to yourself and celebrate every step forward.
13. **Be Patient**: Changes take time. Focus on being consistent.
14. **Create Exercise Cues**: Set up triggers that remind you to exercise, like seeing your sneakers (Harvard | School of Public Health, 2013).

Of course, you don't have to try all these tips but choose some that work for you. Those, along with other task and goal management tips you've learned so far will set you up to have a proper exercise routine daily.

Don't Underestimate the Power of Sleep

When puberty hits, people with ADHD are more likely to have shorter sleep cycles, trouble falling asleep and staying asleep, and a bigger risk of developing a sleep disorder (Pacheco, 2022). Danielle studied the science of sleep and wants to emphasize its importance to adults with ADHD. Before we go into more details, imagine the following scenario:

You've had a restless night, tossing and turning, and now you're facing your workday. Because of your ADHD, this lack of sleep isn't just tiring; it feels like you're wading through mud. Your thoughts scatter, focusing on a task feels like a Herculean effort, and every little distraction pulls you away. In contrast, after a good night's sleep, it's like the fog lifts; your thoughts align, tasks seem manageable, and your day flows smoother.

Danielle explains that sleep is key because it regulates neurotransmitters in the brain, which is crucial for managing ADHD symptoms. Picture neurotransmitters as tiny messengers in your brain, carrying signals between cells, much like boats crossing a river. These signals influence everything from mood and energy levels to focus. So, good sleep helps keep these vital messengers working well, impacting how you feel, think, and act.

It's during deep sleep that our brain processes the day's experiences, balances mood-regulating chemicals like serotonin and dopamine, and resets our stress response. Inadequate sleep, on the other hand, can disrupt this delicate balance, leading to heightened impulsivity, decreased concentration, and exacerbated ADHD symptoms. Prioritizing sleep is like giving your brain the tools it needs to tackle ADHD challenges more effectively.

Poor sleep quality doesn't just leave you feeling tired; it can exacerbate the symptoms of ADHD. Adults with ADHD who suffer from sleep deprivation may experience increased irritability, restlessness, and difficulty in processing information. This can sometimes be mistaken for mood disorders, blurring the line between ADHD symptoms and the effects of poor sleep. The lack of restful sleep can amplify feelings of being overwhelmed and frustrated, making even routine tasks feel more challenging.

Additionally, it may lead to increased dependence on stimulants like caffeine, which can further disrupt sleep patterns and create a vicious cycle of sleeplessness and heightened ADHD symptoms.

To combat these issues, establishing a consistent bedtime routine and practicing good sleep hygiene can make a significant difference. Gradual changes to your sleep habits can include:

- Reducing sugar, caffeine, and alcohol intake before bed.
- Limiting screen time to about an hour before sleep.
- Avoid intense activities or projects in the evening.
- Designating the bed as a place reserved for sleep and relaxation.
- Incorporating regular exercise and exposure to sunlight during the day.
- Creating a calming bedtime ritual, like reading or taking a bath.
- Keeping the bedroom environment conducive to sleep: dark, cool, and quiet.
- Setting consistent sleep and wake times.
- Considering the use of a weighted blanket for added comfort.

By prioritizing and optimizing your sleep, you can significantly improve your ADHD management, leading to better focus, mood stabilization, and overall quality of life. Remember, sleep isn't just a pause in your day; it's a vital component of your health and well-being.

Mastering Stress Management

It's a typical Tuesday. You've got a big work project, the kids need help with homework, and the house is in total chaos. Your mind races from one task to the next, but focusing feels like trying to catch a runaway train. The noise, the clutter, and the clock ticking away just amp up your stress. It's like every little thing is vying for your attention, and it's exhausting. Sounds familiar? If so, then this is where stress management isn't just helpful; it's a lifeline.

As someone dealing with ADHD, you know that stress can feel like an uninvited guest who just won't leave. But guess what? You can totally learn to manage this pesky visitor. Managing stress isn't just a bonus; it's super important for anyone with ADHD. It's all about turning those big waves of stress into little ripples that you can surf on.

Common Stress Triggers for Someone with ADHD

You know those moments that just get under your skin? For those of us with ADHD, certain things can really crank up the stress (CHADD, n.d.). It could be piles of paperwork, noisy environments, or just trying to keep up with daily demands. Recognizing what sets off your stress is like having a secret map, helping you avoid those stress hotspots or be better prepared when you can't.

Stress Management Techniques

Let's talk about tackling stress head-on! Techniques like deep breathing, mindfulness, and taking little breaks are like secret weapons. Here's a quick breakdown of those techniques:

- **Deep Breathing**: Focus on slow, deep breaths to calm your nervous system.
- **Mindfulness**: Trying to be fully present in the moment without judgment will help break the cycle of overthinking.
- **Time-Outs**: Give yourself permission to take short breaks for mental clarity.

They help you catch your breath when life's whirlwind gets too wild. Think of them as your personal stress-busters, ready to jump into action when things get hectic.

Building Stress Management into Daily Life

Imagine building a cool fortress, but this one's for protecting you from stress. That's what stress management in your daily routine is all about. All you have to do is incorporate the following tips:

- Start with short sessions of mindfulness or deep breathing each day.
- Gradually let these practices become natural responses to stress.
- Use time-outs during moments of overwhelm to reset your focus.

Each little habit you form is like a brick in your fortress, making you stronger against the daily hustle and bustle. Before you know it, these small habits will become your go-to shield against the chaos of ADHD.

Benefits of Stress Management

Now, the real magic happens when you start feeling the benefits of all this stress management. They include the following:

- Regular practice leads to improved focus and emotional balance.
- Helps in managing tasks more effectively and reducing impulsivity.
- Creates a sense of well-being, positively affecting personal and professional life.

It's like giving your brain a supercharge, helping you focus better and stay more balanced emotionally. Practicing these techniques regularly is like leveling up in a game, where you become more skilled at handling whatever ADHD throws your way.

Activity: Create a Self-Care Calendar

As you wrap up this chapter, why not embark on a transformative journey by creating your very own self-care calendar? It's super easy, I promise! When you follow the steps below, you'll have a calendar that not only helps you prioritize self-care but also becomes a delightful and relaxing activity in itself.

Step 1: Pick Your Canvas. Start with a blank calendar that resonates with you—whether it's a simple dollar store find or something that sparks joy. Your calendar is a personal reflection of your journey.

Step 2: List Your Self-Care. Consider self-care practices that connect with you. Explore diverse activities for your well-being, drawing inspiration from various sources. Align some months with specific themes or occasions.

Step 3: Add Art and Color. Let your creativity shine with doodles and colors around your chosen activities. Whether vibrant or minimalist, let your artistic expression bring joy to your calendar.

Step 4: Enjoy the Process. Crafting your self-care calendar should be therapeutic. Take your time, and relish each moment without rushing. Consider completing one month at a time for inspired and mindful choices.

Step 5: Keep Inspired. If you enjoy the process, extend it over days or months. Let changing seasons or evolving inspirations shape your self-care calendar content.

So go ahead, have fun, and design a self-care calendar that's uniquely yours. It's a wonderful way to prioritize self-care and bring a little extra joy into your life. Happy creating!

Self-Care Ideas for Your Calendar:

If you're seeking inspiration for your self-care activities, explore the following ideas:

- Take a relaxing bath
- Read a book for pleasure
- Light a comforting candle
- Enjoy a peaceful walk
- Plant some flowers
- Spend quality time with your pets
- Savor a cup of tea
- Visit your favorite café
- Complete a personal project
- Organize your living space
- Bake delicious cookies
- Try a new recipe
- Connect with friends and loved ones
- Engage in a new hobby
- Explore artistic activities like painting
- Practice morning yoga
- Cultivate gratitude with a thankful list
- Volunteer for a cause
- Learn a new language greeting
- Journal your thoughts and experiences
- Sing in the shower
- Dance in the kitchen
- Express love to someone special
- Stay hydrated and nourished
- Take vitamins for well-being

- Indulge in a face mask or hair mask
- Thrift shop for hidden treasures
- Watch your favorite movie
- Make a refreshing smoothie
- Learn to sew or knit
- Listen to uplifting music
- Create a playlist of happy tunes
- Reflect on your dreams and aspirations
- Find a mantra for daily inspiration
- Read positive quotes
- Declutter by donating unused items (Elizabeth, 2021).

May your self-care calendar be a beautiful reminder of your dedication to taking care of yourself. Let it guide you on a journey of mindfulness and happiness. Enjoy creating it!!

Achieving your goals takes more than just setting them. In the next chapter, we'll talk more about how your lifestyle choices like diet, exercise, sleep, and stress management can be game changers.

Chapter 7

The Power of a Growth Mindset

Have you ever felt like you're stuck in a maze with no way out? Maybe it was a problem at work, a personal goal, or managing your ADHD where you couldn't see a way forward. We've all been there. This feeling often comes down to our 'mindset' - how we view ourselves and our abilities (Cherry, 2022).

In this chapter, we will explore how shifting from a fixed mindset (thinking your abilities are carved in stone) to a growth mindset (believing you can grow and improve) can be a game-changer, especially when managing ADHD. We'll dive into real-life examples and hands-on activities to help you make this important shift. Imagine turning "I can't" into "I just haven't mastered it yet." That's the power of a growth mindset, and it's going to open up a whole new world for you.

Understanding Fixed and Growth Mindsets

When we talk about ADHD, we often focus on the external stuff, like medications, therapies, and daily routines. But what about the way we think? That's where fixed and growth mindsets come in. They're pretty big deals in how we handle life, especially with ADHD. Let's break it down.

Fixed Mindset: A Limiting View

A fixed mindset is like believing your brain's abilities are set in stone. It's thinking that the talents and smarts you have now are all you're ever going to have. For someone with ADHD, this mindset can be a bit of a trap.

For example, imagine you're at work, and there's this huge project that needs organizing – something that's usually a challenge for you because of your ADHD. With a fixed mindset, you might think, "I've never been good at organizing because of my ADHD, and that's never going to change." This thought can stop you in your tracks. You might not even try to find new ways to tackle the project or improve your organizing skills because you believe you're just not cut out for it.

This kind of mindset can make you feel stuck and unable to change or grow. It's like you're in a room with doors to new opportunities, but you believe they're all locked, so you never even try the handles.

Growth Mindset: A Path to New Possibilities

The growth mindset means you believe you can improve and develop your abilities with effort and persistence. It's seeing your brain as a muscle that gets stronger the more you use it. For someone with ADHD, this mindset transforms challenges into opportunities for growth.

For example, imagine you're struggling to stay focused in a long meeting – a typical ADHD hurdle. With a growth mindset, you shift from thinking, "I'm just bad at this," to "I'm figuring out how to improve." So, you try new techniques, like taking notes or setting mini-goals for staying engaged. This new approach transforms a challenging situation into an opportunity to boost your focusing skills.

Carol Dweck, the psychologist who introduced this concept, offers a wealth of insights on how this mindset can significantly impact our lives (Dweck, 2015). Adopting a growth mindset doesn't mean you'll suddenly find everything easy. It means you recognize your potential to learn and grow. It's about celebrating the small victories and viewing setbacks as part of the learning process. With this mindset, every challenge becomes a stepping stone to becoming a better version of yourself.

What is Your Current Mindset?

Knowing whether you have a fixed or growth mindset can be a game-changer, especially for adults with ADHD. Here's how you can tell where you stand:

Signs You Might Be in a Fixed Mindset:

- Avoiding new projects because you fear failure.
- Feeling defensive when receiving feedback or criticism.
- Comparing yourself negatively to others who seem to manage their ADHD better.
- Believing that your ADHD symptoms are unchangeable and define you.
- Giving up easily when ADHD-related challenges arise (Smith, 2020).

Signs You're Embracing a Growth Mindset:

- Viewing ADHD-related challenges as opportunities to learn and grow.
- Seeking feedback as a tool for improvement, not as a personal attack.
- Celebrating the successes of others and finding inspiration in them.
- Acknowledging your ADHD while also believing in your ability to improve your coping strategies.
- Persisting through setbacks and viewing them as part of the learning process (Smith, 2020).

The first step in moving towards a more growth-oriented mindset is becoming aware of these signs. It allows you to understand where you are now and how you can start shifting towards a perspective that embraces challenges and personal development.

Whether you're more inclined towards a fixed mindset or a growth mindset can significantly influence your journey with ADHD. It's not about ignoring the challenges but about reframing how you perceive and tackle them. Accept the challenges, learn from them, and keep moving forward on your personal growth journey.

The Benefits of a Growth Mindset in ADHD Management

Alright, so you're familiar with the difference between a fixed and growth mindset, right? Now, let's see why adopting a growth mindset could be a total game-changer for you, according to a mindset coaching company called Inner Drive (InnerDrive, n.d.). This isn't just about a positive attitude; it's about real, tangible benefits that can make managing your ADHD a whole lot smoother. Stick with me, and let's explore how this mindset shift can transform how you handle those ADHD challenges.

1. Stress Reduction

First off, a growth mindset can seriously dial down your stress levels. When you start seeing ADHD-related challenges as hurdles you can actually jump over (with some practice), the whole stress game changes. It's about turning those "Oh no, not this again" moments into "Okay, what can I learn from this?" situations.

Picture this – you're trying to cook dinner, but you keep getting distracted and forgetting ingredients. Instead of getting stressed and thinking, "I can't even cook a simple meal right," a growth mindset helps you take a deep breath and think, "Let's slow down. Maybe I can lay out all the ingredients first or use a recipe app to keep track." This change in approach turns a chaotic kitchen experience into a more organized and stress-free cooking session.

2. Building Resilience

Next up is resilience. This is your bounce-back ability. Didn't nail that new organization method on the first try? No worries. With a growth mindset, you're more like, "Alright, let's tweak this and give it another shot." It's about being more Teflon and less Velcro when setbacks come your way.

Let's say you've been trying to use a digital planner to stay organized, but it's not clicking for you. With a fixed mindset, you might give up, thinking you're just not cut out for the organization. But with a growth mindset, you think, "Maybe this tool isn't right for me. Let's try a different approach, like a traditional paper planner or a different app." This resilience keeps you experimenting and learning until you find what works best for your unique ADHD challenges.

3. Self-Regulation and Confidence Boost

Then, there's the boost to self-regulation and self-esteem. Managing your reactions, staying focused, and not letting emotions run the show – that's self-regulation. And as you get better at this, guess what? Your confidence gets a major lift, too. It's like learning to ride the waves instead of being knocked over by them.

You're in a meeting and realize you've drifted off and missed important information. In the past, this might have led to self-criticism and a loss of confidence. But with improved self-regulation, you gently remind yourself that it's okay and discreetly ask a colleague for a recap or check the meeting minutes later. This approach not only helps you manage the situation but also boosts your confidence in handling similar situations in the future.

4. Effective Habit Formation

With a growth mindset, you're also more likely to adopt effective habits. Think of it like collecting the best tools for your ADHD toolbox. You're not just trying things willy-nilly; you're strategically picking methods and habits that really work for you.

For example, you're trying to have a morning routine that allows you to start your day on the right foot. Instead of randomly trying every tip you come across, you use a growth mindset to methodically test different routines, like exercising in the morning, meditating, or creating a to-do list the night before. Over time, you find a combination that really clicks, turning these actions into effective habits that make your mornings, and thus your entire day, more ADHD-friendly.

5. Enhanced Problem-Solving Skills

And here's the fifth big win: better problem-solving skills. A growth mindset equips you to tackle problems more creatively and effectively. You start to look at challenges with a "How can I solve this?" attitude rather than an "I can't deal with this" mindset. It's about turning problems into puzzles that you're eager to solve.

Imagine you're struggling to keep your home tidy, which is a common challenge with ADHD. The clutter seems over-whelming, and you often think, "I just can't keep this place organized." With a growth mindset, you start to tackle the problem creatively, like setting a timer for 10 minutes each day to do a quick clean-up or designating specific spots for commonly misplaced items. This strategy turns the over-whelming task of organizing your home into manageable, bite-sized actions, making your living space more comfortable and less cluttered.

So there you have it — five solid ways a growth mindset can seriously upgrade your ADHD management game. When you lean into a growth mindset, you also start to value effective strategies more. It's like finding the best tools for a job. And guess what? You also become more open to feedback. Instead of hearing it as criticism, you see it as helpful advice to do better next time.

Adopting a growth mindset is not about pretending that managing ADHD is easy. It's about changing how you view and tackle the challenges. It's like shifting from "I can't do this" to "I'm learning how to do this." You start to see every challenge as a stepping stone and every effort as a victory, no matter how small.

Making the Shift: Strategies and Exercises

Going from a fixed mindset to one of growth can feel like a big leap, especially if you've been viewing the world through a fixed lens for a while. But fear not! I've got some strategies and exercises that can help make this shift more manageable and a regular part of your daily life.

1. **Assess Your Current Mindset:** Let's start by figuring out where you stand. Do you often find yourself stuck in fixed mindset thinking? Acknowledging this is your starting point. It's like knowing your location before you start a journey.
2. **Define Your Motivation:** 2. Why do you want to develop a growth mindset? Maybe it's to handle your

ADHD better or to feel more confident in tackling new challenges. Defining these motivations will help you to remain focused, especially when things get tough.

3. **Seek Inspiration:** Talk to people who embody a growth mindset. Hearing how others have embraced this way of thinking can be incredibly inspiring. It's like having real-life examples that this mindset is achievable and beneficial.

4. **Learn About Brain Plasticity:** Understanding how the brain works can be a powerful motivator. Dive into the world of neuroplasticity to see how capable your brain is of learning and adapting. It's a scientific way of proving to yourself that change is possible (Wooll, 2021).

5. **Reframe Failure:** Start seeing failure not as a roadblock but as part of the learning process. Remember, every successful person has faced setbacks. It's how they responded to these setbacks that made all the difference.

6. **Acknowledge Your Limits:** It's okay to recognize that some things might be more challenging for you. This understanding helps you set realistic goals and dedicate the right amount of effort where it's needed.

7. **Watch Your Language:** Pay attention to how you talk about yourself and others. Swap out self-deprecating language for more positive, growth-oriented phrases. Instead of saying, "I'm no good at this," try, "I'm not great at this yet" (Cunff, 2020).

These strategies will help your mindset go from fixed to being growth-orientated. But they can be a bit scary, especially for someone with ADHD. So, how can you make these part of your daily routine? Here are some suggestions:

1. **Daily Reflections:** Spend a few minutes each day reflecting on your thoughts and actions. Did you approach situations with a fixed or growth mindset?
2. **Set Small Goals:** Break down big challenges into smaller, achievable goals. Celebrate each small victory as a sign of your growing abilities.
3. **Mindset Journaling:** Keep a journal where you write down fixed mindset thoughts and then reframe them into growth mindset perspectives.
4. **Mindful Meditation:** Practice mindfulness to help you stay present and aware of your mindset.

By incorporating these strategies and exercises into your daily routine, you'll gradually find yourself adopting a more growth-oriented mindset. Remember, it's a journey, not a race. Each step you take is progress towards a more adaptable, resilient you.

Activity: Discover Your Mindset

Ready to find out where your mindset stands? The quiz below will help you identify your current mindset and offer tips on shifting towards a growth mindset. Just answer with a 'Yes' or 'No' to each statement:

1. **Challenges**: When I face a difficult problem, I tend to give up easily.
2. **Effort**: I believe putting in a lot of effort to learn something new is not really worth it.
3. **Mistakes**: When I make a mistake, I feel like it's a failure rather than a learning opportunity.
4. **Feedback**: I often feel defensive or discouraged when I receive constructive criticism.
5. **Success of Others**: When others succeed, I feel jealous or threatened rather than inspired.
6. **Abilities**: I think my ability to succeed in new tasks is predetermined, and I can't do much to change it.

Scoring Your Quiz:

- **Mostly 'Yes' Answers**: This suggests you might lean towards a fixed mindset. You may view your abilities and potential as static, which can limit your growth and learning.
- **A mix of 'Yes' and 'No' Answers**: You're likely in between mindsets. You may recognize the value of growth and learning but sometimes feel held back by fixed mindset tendencies.
- **Mostly 'No' Answers**: You're already embracing a growth mindset! You see challenges and mistakes as opportunities to grow and learn.

Regardless of where you are on the spectrum, you can cultivate a growth mindset with the following tips:

- Embrace challenges.
- Value effort.
- Learn from mistakes.
- Welcome feedback.
- Celebrate others' success.
- Believe in growth.

Remember that adopting a growth mindset isn't just about personal development. It's about having a powerful tool that can transform your relationships, too. When you start seeing challenges as opportunities and embrace growth, it positively impacts how you interact and connect with others. This change in perspective can make a difference in understanding and navigating the dynamics of relationships, especially when living with ADHD. Excited for more insights? In Chapter 8, we'll explore the world of relationships and ADHD, discovering ways to foster stronger, more understanding connections with the people in your life.

Chapter 8

Relationship Dynamics

P icture this: You're rushing to a dinner date because you lost track of time, a familiar struggle for those with ADHD. Your partner feels hurt and neglected, and the situation quickly turns into a misunderstanding rooted in ADHD-related issues. This is a common scenario that highlights the intricate relationship between ADHD and relationship dynamics.

In this chapter, we'll look at the unique ways ADHD can impact relationships and provide practical tools to improve communication. You'll discover strategies to navigate common challenges such as forgetfulness, rejection-sensitive dysphoria, and misunderstandings. We aim to equip you with actionable advice to establish healthy boundaries, resolve conflicts, and foster understanding and empathy in your relationships.

How ADHD Affects Relationships

Living with ADHD can often feel like a never-ending juggling act. Let's take Jackson as an example. He has ADHD, and sometimes, he gets so hyperfocused on tasks at work that he once completely forgot about his own anniversary dinner plans. But on the flip side, his spontaneous ideas and his unique perspective on the world bring a special vibrancy to his relationships. This combination of forgetfulness and creative thinking shapes how he interacts with his partners, friends, and family.

You know, when it comes to relationships, ADHD brings both challenges and benefits. According to Carolina Wellness Psychiatry, these challenges can become even more pronounced if one or both partners have ADHD (Carolina Wellness Psychiatry, n.d.). So, let's dive deeper into those challenges and benefits.

The Challenges

Because of your symptoms, you might have some unique challenges when it comes to your relationship, like the following:

Forgetfulness is a common issue in ADHD, often leading to missed appointments or overlooked responsibilities. This can sometimes make partners feel neglected or undervalued.

Impulsivity, another ADHD trait, might manifest in making large purchases without discussing it with a partner, potentially leading to conflicts over finances.

Attention Issues can also pose challenges. Difficulty in paying attention to your partner or missing non-verbal cues can leave them feeling unheard or unimportant.

Organizational Struggles can create tension, especially if the burden of household chores falls more on one partner.

Emotional Regulation can be tricky. The highs and lows typical of ADHD can be hard for partners to keep up with, leading to misunderstandings or arguments.

See if you relate to this challenge: You might find yourself interrupting your partner mid-conversation because a new thought pops into your head. While your ideas are valuable, this habit can leave your partner feeling unheard and frustrated, straining the flow of your communication.

The Benefits

On the flip side, ADHD can also bring unique strengths to relationships:

Creativity and Energy: Your boundless energy can inject excitement and fresh ideas into your relationships, keeping them dynamic and engaging.

Passion and Spontaneity: Living in the moment is one of your superpowers. This brings a zest for life that enlivens any activity, making your time with others fun and spontaneous.

Open-mindedness: Your experience of seeing the world differently makes you open to new ideas and perspectives. This not only makes you a supportive partner but also helps you embrace diverse viewpoints in all your relationships.

Unique Perspectives: Your ability to hyperfocus means you can dive deep into hobbies and interests. This trait often leads to shared passions and deeper connections with those around you.

Empathy and Understanding: You have a heightened sense of empathy, which is invaluable in understanding and supporting your partner and others close to you (Frampton, 2023).

For example, here's a relatable benefit you might have experienced: You might often surprise your partner with spontaneous date ideas or creative solutions to everyday problems, injecting excitement and novelty into your relationship. This spontaneity keeps things lively and demonstrates your ability to make ordinary moments extraordinary.

Relationships, whether they're romantic, familial, or platonic, can be quite complex. It's important to understand how ADHD influences these dynamics, as it can help us build stronger and more empathetic connections. Throughout this section, we've delved into the challenges and strengths that ADHD can bring to relationships. We aim to provide a balanced perspective that recognizes the difficulties while celebrating the unique qualities that individuals with ADHD contribute to their connections.

Communication Tips

If you or your partner has ADHD, it's super important to understand how it can affect communication in relationships. Sometimes, you might forget to reply to texts or important dates. It's not about not caring, but ADHD can make focusing tough. Also, you might feel super sensitive to criticism or rejection, which is totally normal for ADHD but can make talking about problems a bit tricky. And hey, misunderstandings happen, especially if ADHD isn't well understood (Hughes, 2023). Remember, learning about ADHD and creating a space where everyone feels safe to talk can really help make your relationship stronger.

Improving communication in a relationship, especially where ADHD is involved, is an effective way to feel connected and understood. There are several strategies you can follow to enhance the way you and your partner communicate, which will lead to a healthier and more balanced relationship. Here's a quick rundown:

1. **Active Listening:** This is all about really tuning into what your partner is saying without planning your response while they're still talking. It's like giving your full attention to a favorite movie, absorbing every word.

2. **Slowing Down Conversations:** When things get heated, try taking a breath and slowing down the pace. It's like driving through a scenic route instead of

racing on the highway - you get to appreciate and understand each other's points more clearly.

3. **Validation:** Acknowledge your partner's feelings and views. You don't have to agree, but understanding and acknowledging their perspective shows that you respect them. Think of it as saying, "I see where you're coming from," even if you're on different pages.

4. **Balancing Status:** Remember, you're equals in this relationship. Avoid falling into a parent-child dynamic where one dictates, and the other listens. Instead, ensure both of you have equal opportunities to speak and be heard.

5. **Focus on One Topic:** If conversations tend to bounce around, try to stick to one subject at a time. It's like completing one puzzle before starting another - it helps in resolving issues more effectively.

6. **Shared Power Through Belief:** Sharing power means believing in each other's experiences, thoughts, and feelings. It's not about agreeing on everything but about validating each other's reality.

When you implement these strategies, they can help create a more harmonious and understanding atmosphere in your relationship. It's about building a partnership where both of you feel heard, respected, and valued. Remember, good communication is a journey, not a destination, so keep learning and growing together!

Okay, but what about difficult conversations? Well, learning how to effectively participate in these discussions not only enhances understanding between partners but also contributes to the overall success of the relationship. Here's how to approach such conversations:

1. **Set Clear Expectations:** Identify what you aim to achieve.
2. **Prepare Both Sides:** Give your partner time to prepare for the discussion.
3. **Stay Positive and Honest:** Keep the conversation constructive.
4. **Keep Calm and Respectful:** Control emotions and remain respectful.
5. **Practice Active Listening:** Understand and validate your partner's perspective.
6. **Stay on Topic:** Focus on the current issue.
7. **Set a Goal or Agreement:** Work towards a resolution or plan.
8. **Be Accountable:** Follow up and adjust plans as needed (Connect Couples Therapy, 2022).

Remember, having these conversations is a part of growing together in a relationship. By following these steps, you can approach difficult topics with more confidence and understanding.

Conflict Resolution

Conflict resolution is super important in any relationship, especially when one partner has ADHD. We know that ADHD can bring some unique challenges, like impulsivity and difficulty managing emotions, which can lead to more frequent and intense conflicts. But don't worry; there are strategies tailored just for you to help resolve these conflicts!

Let's dive into four common conflicts that any relationship can face and see what we can do to resolve them.

1. **Conflict Over Household Chores:** We understand that ADHD can make it tough to stay organized and complete tasks, which can create an imbalance in household chores. A shared responsibility chart is one way to avoid this conflict altogether. This chart can provide a clear structure and help both partners understand their roles. Additionally, using reminders or alarms for task completion can assist in ensuring that chores are done, reducing conflicts in this area.

2. **Financial Disagreements:** We know that impulsivity associated with ADHD might lead to spontaneous spending, which can strain your finances. To tackle this, it's a great idea to develop a joint budgeting plan. This way, both partners can manage their spending and make unified decisions about their finances. Having regular financial discussions can also help keep everyone on the same page.

3. **Parenting Style Differences:** ADHD-related challenges can sometimes lead to differing views on parenting, which can cause conflict. It's important to openly discuss and align parenting strategies. By doing so, you can find common ground and work together as a team. Remember, presenting a united front and supporting each other's decisions in front of the children is crucial for consistency.

4. **Attention and Affection Needs:** We understand that ADHD can affect consistent attention and affection, which might leave a partner feeling neglected. To address this, it's helpful to establish regular check-ins or schedule date nights. This ensures dedicated time for each partner and helps maintain a sense of connection and value in the relationship.

Remember, effective communication and conflict resolution are key to managing these common challenges in relationships where ADHD is a factor. By understanding the underlying reasons for conflicts and working together on solutions, you can greatly improve your relationship dynamics. You've got this!

The Importance of Active Listening and Emotional Regulation

When it comes to resolving conflicts, active listening, and emotional regulation are key. So, what does that mean? Well, active listening means really focusing on your partner, showing empathy, and understanding their perspective. I know it can be tough, especially with ADHD, but making a conscious effort to stay engaged in the conversation can make a big difference.

Now, let's talk about emotional regulation. ADHD can make it harder to control our emotions, which can sometimes make conflicts worse. But fear not! I have some techniques you can learn to manage your emotions. Taking deep breaths and recognizing triggers are just a couple of examples. These skills not only help prevent conflicts from escalating but also create a more understanding and supportive environment in your relationship. So, keep practicing, and remember, you've got this!

Setting Boundaries

By setting boundaries, you will maintain a healthy and fulfilling relationship, especially if you have ADHD. It matters for a few different reasons. First off, let's talk about preserving individuality. It's so important to have personal space and interests within a relationship. Boundaries help you have a healthy sense of self while still being part of a partnership. They give you the freedom to pursue your own passions and grow as an individual.

Clear boundaries can be a game-changer when it comes to preventing misunderstandings and conflicts. When both you and your partner know and respect each other's limits, it becomes easier to navigate disagreements. By having those boundaries in place, you create a framework for open and respectful communication. So, when conflicts arise, you can address them more amicably and constructively.

Last but not least, let's talk about stress reduction. Managing stress is crucial, especially for individuals with ADHD. Boundaries provide a structure that helps reduce the likelihood of feeling overwhelmed by the demands of a relationship. By setting boundaries around your time, energy, and commitments, you can create a more manageable and balanced environment. Remember, it's okay to prioritize self-care and ensure that your needs are met.

So, embrace the power of boundaries in your relationships. And if you're not exactly sure how to do that, don't worry. Below are tips for setting and maintaining boundaries and how to communicate them clearly to your partner.

Tips for Setting and Maintaining Boundaries:

1. **Self-Reflection:** Take time to identify your own needs, triggers, and what makes you comfortable or uncomfortable in the relationship. Understanding your boundaries is the first step in setting them.
2. **Open Communication:** Initiate an open conversation with your partner about the importance of boundaries where both of you are completely honest. Explain how they can benefit both of you and foster a healthier relationship.
3. **Start Small:** Begin by setting boundaries in less emotionally charged situations. This can help you practice communication and establish trust with your partner.
4. **Be Specific:** Clearly articulate your boundaries. Use specific examples to illustrate your points. For

instance, instead of saying, "I need more space," say, "I'd appreciate an hour of alone time in the evenings."

5. **Active Listening:** Allow your partner to share their boundaries in a safe, non-judgmental space. Then, listen actively to their needs and concerns and validate their feelings.

6. **Respect Each Other:** Respect is key to maintaining boundaries. Both partners must agree to adhere to the established boundaries and support each other in maintaining them.

Communicating Your Boundaries Clearly:

1. **Choose the Right Time:** Find a quiet, comfortable moment to discuss boundaries. Avoid doing so during an argument or when tensions are high.

2. **Use "I" Statements:** Frame your boundaries as personal needs. Instead of saying, "You should do this," say, "I feel better when..."

3. **Be Patient:** Understand that it may take time for your partner to adjust to your boundaries. Patience and compromise are essential for a successful transition.

4. **Regular Check-Ins:** Periodically revisit your boundaries. As life evolves, your needs may change, so it's essential to ensure that your boundaries remain relevant and effective.

5. **Seek Support:** Consider seeking the assistance of a therapist or counselor, especially if you encounter difficulties in establishing or maintaining boundaries.

By setting and communicating boundaries effectively, individuals with ADHD can cultivate healthier, more fulfilling relationships with their partners, reducing stress and promoting overall well-being.

Activity: Role-Play Difficult Conversations

Okay, so you've read all about how ADHD can twist up communication in relationships. How about we try something a bit different to wrap up this chapter? Let's role-play a difficult conversation. It's like a rehearsal for real life and can be super helpful for us ADHD folks.

Setting the Scene

1. **Pick Your Characters**: Grab a buddy for this. One of you is 'you,' and the other is playing the person you're having this tricky talk with. Got a third friend? Awesome, they can watch and give feedback.
2. **Choose Your Battle**: Think of a typical ADHD mishap, like spacing out on a promise or getting the wires crossed on what your partner asked you to do.
3. **What's the Aim?**: If you're playing 'you,' your mission is to tackle the issue while keeping cool and collected. The other person? They should react how they think the real person would.

How to Play It Out

- **Ditch the 'Always' and 'Never'**: When you're getting your point across, skip words like 'always' or 'never.' Trust me, they can make things heat up fast.
- **Stick to the Script**: Focus on what needs to change, and don't get sidetracked by the nitty-gritty details.
- **Keep It Real**: The person playing your partner or friend should react in a way that's true to life, but let's not go full soap opera. We're aiming for real talk here.
- **Post-Game Analysis**: After you're done, chat about what hit the mark and what could've gone smoother (Hogan, 2019).

Reflecting on It

Post-role-play, have a little debrief:

- Which bits felt right and kept things on track?
- How did it feel to manage the convo with your new growth mindset?
- If you had a third person watching, what nuggets of wisdom did they drop?

Now, take what you've learned from this pretend play and use it in your actual conversations. Dealing with communication in relationships, especially when ADHD is in the mix, is all about understanding, patience, and growing from each chat.

Chapter 8 is a wrap! We've tackled relationship dynamics, especially when ADHD is in the mix. But guess what? The skills we've covered here aren't just for your personal life; they're gold in the workplace, too.

Chapter 9 is next, and it's all about personal growth at work. Those communication strategies, resilience-building, and understanding you've honed? They're your secret weapons for professional success. Whether you're navigating coworker relationships or conquering workplace challenges, the skills you've acquired here are about to shine in a new setting. Are you ready?

Let Others Know That ADHD Can Be a Superpower

"The best way to think of ADHD is not as a mental disorder, but as a collection of traits and tendencies that define a way of being in the world."

— *Edward Hallowell*

In the introduction, I mentioned that before developing a greater awareness of ADHD and how it affected my perception of the world, I always saw it as a problem that needed fixing. Understanding that it was a lifelong companion was a revelation—a reminder that navigating ADHD starts by accepting that it may bring challenges, while also knowing that there is plenty you can do to mitigate its complexities and harness its strengths.

I hope that the information you have found in these pages makes you feel like embracing your uniqueness and helping you see the many positive traits that come along with the challenges. Throughout the book, you will continue to find a host of practical tips that will help make everything from completing daily tasks to relationships with others smoother and more enriching.

By this stage of your reading, you know the importance of identifying your triggers, embracing a growth mindset, and committing to a small but highly effective list of actions (such as goal-setting and time management). If you have started adopting these strategies and they are making a difference to your life, I hope you can share your opinion with others.

By leaving a review of this book on Amazon, you'll help other people who are looking for practical strategies to harness the best things about ADHD and limit the effects of its biggest challenges.

Let others know that it is possible to work with instead of against ADHD.

Thank you so much for your support. It makes an incredible difference.

Scan the QR code below to leave your review!

Chapter 9

Personal Development in the Workplace

I magine you've just landed your dream job, but during your first week, a crucial deadline slips through your fingers. The familiar weight of ADHD symptoms feels like a sinking ship, threatening your new role. But what if this isn't the end of your story? What if ADHD could become your strongest ally in forging a successful career path? This chapter is here to turn that 'what if' into a reality.

In this chapter, we're diving into the unique challenges and opportunities that come with ADHD in the workplace. We'll provide practical advice on managing ADHD symptoms, honing your professional skills, and navigating the complexities of workplace relationships. Our goal? To empower you to transform ADHD from a hurdle into a stepping stone for your career success.

Managing ADHD Symptoms for Career Success

Picture this: You're stepping into the professional world with ADHD. It's not just about nailing the job or scaling up the career ladder; it's about playing to your strengths and skillfully handling the symptoms that might hold you back. This chapter is all about empowering you to turn ADHD into a powerful tool for career success.

How Your ADHD Symptoms Can Affect Job Performance

Your ADHD comes with its own set of challenges that might show up at work. Maybe you find it hard to stay focused or manage your time. These can lead to tricky situations like missing deadlines or getting tangled in multitasking. But here's the thing – with the right approach, you can navigate these waters successfully.

Coping with Your ADHD Symptoms at Work

Tackling ADHD at work means finding strategies and tools that gel with your unique way of working. It's not just about overcoming hurdles; it's about crafting a work style that plays to your strengths. Let's explore some tactics that can really boost your performance:

1. **Task Management Tools:** Think of these as your digital sidekicks, keeping you on track with tasks and deadlines.
2. **Structured Routines:** A regular routine can be a game-changer, giving you a sense of predictability and structure.
3. **Break Down Tasks:** Facing a mountain of work? Break it into smaller hills. It's all about making big projects manageable.
4. **Regular Breaks:** Short breaks aren't just downtime; they're recharge moments to keep your energy and focus sharp.

Imagine you're juggling multiple projects, and it feels like you're trying to catch falling leaves in a windstorm. By adopting these steps, you'll have a digital net to catch those leaves, turning chaos into order. This isn't just about meeting deadlines; it's about feeling in control and less frazzled, which makes you more confident and effective at work.

Prioritizing Tasks to Sidestep Overwhelm

Getting your tasks in order is super important for you. It helps keep that feeling of being swamped in check and points your attention where it's needed most. In the hustle of the workplace, this skill is your secret weapon.

1. **The Brain Dump:** Get all your tasks down on paper. It's like clearing the fog in your mind to see what's important.

2. **Categorize and Prioritize:** Sort your tasks by urgency and importance. Tackle the biggies first.
3. **Set Realistic Goals:** Aim for what's achievable, not the moon. Setting realistic goals keeps stress at bay.
4. **Flexibility:** Build some wiggle room into your schedule for those curveballs life throws at you.

Think of a time when your workday felt like a game of Tetris, with tasks piling up faster than you could handle. By prioritizing your tasks, you're essentially clearing those rows before they hit the top. It's about knowing which blocks to place first to avoid a pile-up. This strategy helps you stay calm and collected and impress your colleagues and bosses with your efficiency and focus.

Tips for Professional Development

I get it; carving out a successful professional path when you have ADHD can feel like a whole different ball game compared to what works for neurotypical folks. Traditional career tactics might not always click with your unique ADHD brain wiring. But here's the deal – your ADHD doesn't have to be a roadblock. In fact, it can be your superpower once you figure out how to use it to your advantage. Let's explore some ways you can do just that.

- **Networking:** Be yourself, be genuine, and remember it's about helping others as much as they can help you. Platforms like LinkedIn are great for making connections.

- **Continuous Learning:** Dive into online courses, workshops, or podcasts that spark your interest. It's about nurturing your curiosity and staying at the top of your game.
- **Seeking Mentorship:** Look for someone who understands your ADHD challenges and goals. Open up about your ADHD so they can offer tailored advice. A mentor-mentee relationship is a partnership for mutual respect, learning, and growth.

So, there you have it. Networking, continuous learning, and mentorship aren't just buzzwords; they're your tools for turning ADHD into your career advantage. Embrace them, and watch how they transform your professional journey.

Navigating Workplace Relationships

You know, good connections with your coworkers and bosses are super important, whether you've got ADHD or not. These relationships can make your job a lot more enjoyable, foster a sense of belonging, and even help you climb the career ladder. It's all about creating a network of support that helps you tackle challenges and celebrate successes.

Building Good Relationships at Work

Now, building these relationships takes some elbow grease, especially when you're juggling ADHD. It's a bit like learning to dance; initially, you might step on a few toes, but soon you'll be moving in sync. For instance, have you ever had a moment where a simple miscommunication led to a workplace blunder? Smooth, clear communication can turn moments like these into opportunities for teamwork and understanding.

1. **Communication is Key:** Clear communication prevents misunderstandings and builds trust. How to do it: After meetings, try summarizing key points and sending them in an email to involved team members to ensure everyone's on the same page.
2. **Show Appreciation:** Acknowledging others' efforts creates a positive work environment. Drop a note or email saying thanks, or give a shout-out in your next team meeting.
3. **Be Reliable:** When people know they can count on you, it strengthens your relationships. How to do it: Use reminders and set alarms for deadlines to help you stay on track.
4. **Seek Feedback:** shows that you're open to growth and value others' opinions. How to do it: Schedule regular one-on-ones with your boss or ask for feedback after completing a task.

Smooth, clear communication can turn moments like these into opportunities for teamwork and understanding.

Challenges in Workplace Relationships Due to ADHD

Navigating social dynamics at work is another thing that doesn't come as easily to someone with ADHD. You might miss some signals or get the frequency wrong sometimes. For example, imagine you're in a meeting, and your mind drifts off, missing key points. Or perhaps your impulsivity leads to interrupting others without realizing it. These moments can significantly affect your workplace relationships, but the good news is they're manageable.

1. Missing subtle social cues
2. Struggling with impulsivity
3. Difficulty following long discussions

It's normal to face these challenges, and you're definitely not alone. Many people with ADHD experience similar issues in the workplace. The key is to acknowledge these challenges and actively work on them. By doing so, you'll find that these obstacles become less daunting over time, and you'll learn how to navigate workplace relationships more smoothly. Remember, every challenge you overcome is a step closer to building stronger, more understanding connections with your colleagues.

Reading Social Cues and Signs

Understanding and responding to social cues in the workplace is crucial but can be challenging with ADHD. Here's how you can get better at it:

1. Understand your colleagues' thoughts and feelings by observing their body language and facial expressions during meetings or conversations.

2. Avoid misunderstandings by seeking clarification when you're unsure about a response or social cue.
3. Show that you value your colleagues' opinions and build stronger connections. Focus on the speaker, nod or verbally acknowledge, and repeat to confirm your understanding.

Improving in these areas can make a huge difference in how you connect with your team. It's about being present, attentive, and responsive – key ingredients for positive and effective workplace interactions. Remember, every step towards better communication and understanding is a step towards a more fulfilling professional life.

Disclosing ADHD at Work

Navigating the workplace with ADHD can be a tough decision. You find yourself at a crossroads, trying to figure out if you should disclose your condition to your employer. It's all about weighing the potential for support against the risk of misunderstanding and bias.

Pros and Cons of Telling Your Employer

Considering the advantages and disadvantages of revealing your ADHD at work is really important. It's a choice that can greatly impact your professional life.

Pros	Cons
Access to Accommodations: Disclosing your ADHD can lead to workplace adjustments that help you perform your best.	**Risk of Stigma**: There's the potential for misunderstanding or bias against ADHD.
Improved Understanding: It can foster a supportive environment where your challenges are recognized and accommodated.	**Potential for Bias**: You might face conscious or unconscious bias from colleagues or superiors.
Authenticity: Being open about your ADHD can reduce the stress of hiding your challenges and promote a more authentic work experience.	**Privacy Concerns**: Sharing about your ADHD means opening up about a personal aspect of your life with which you may not feel comfortable.

Guidelines on How and When to Disclose

Deciding when and how to tell your boss about your ADHD at work is kind of like navigating a tricky maze. You have to think carefully and choose the right time. Imagine a situation where your ADHD makes it difficult for you to complete an important project. This could be a good opportunity to talk to your boss about your ADHD, especially if there are accommodations that could help you do better. Here are some guidelines on how and when to disclose:

1. **Know Your Rights:** Equip yourself with knowledge about your legal rights concerning disability disclosure and accommodations.

2. **Timing is Key:** Consider disclosing when you feel ADHD-related support or accommodations would greatly benefit your work.

3. **Prepare Your Case:** Have a clear understanding of the accommodations you need and how they will aid your job performance.

After laying out your strategy, take a moment to assess the atmosphere of your workplace. It's important to feel out whether your environment seems receptive and supportive of such disclosures.

Seeking Accommodations

If you choose to share, asking for accommodations is like building a better work environment that supports you and helps you succeed. It's about making sure your ADHD doesn't hinder your performance, but instead, finding ways to manage it that actually improve your work. So, consider the following:

1. **Be Specific:** Clearly articulate the accommodations you need and why.

2. **Suggest Practical Solutions:** Propose realistic and feasible solutions that can be easily integrated into your work setting.

3. **Follow-up:** Keep communication open with your employer to ensure that the accommodations are implemented effectively.

In conclusion, the decision to disclose your ADHD at work involves carefully balancing your personal needs against the potential professional impact. Whether you decide to disclose or not, remember that your ADHD is a part of your unique professional story and doesn't define your overall capabilities or value in your career.

Work-Life Balance

Work-life balance is basically juggling your job and your personal life in a way that doesn't make you feel like you're constantly dropping one ball or the other. But when you have ADHD, this juggling act can get a bit more complicated. It's like trying to keep all these balls in the air while walking on a balance beam.

Setting boundaries between work and the rest of your life is like drawing a line in the sand. It's about saying, "This is where work ends and my personal time begins." Why is this important? Because when work seeps into every corner of your life, it's like leaving no room for anything else – and that's a recipe for stress and burnout.

1. **Create a Structured Schedule:** Having specific work hours helps keep ADHD symptoms in check and separates work from play.
2. **Designate Workspaces:** A dedicated work area helps your brain switch between 'work mode' and 'chill mode.'

3. **Use Reminders and Alarms:** Think of them as friendly nudges to wrap up work and start focusing on you.

Now, about unplugging and chilling out – it's super important for your work-life balance. It's like giving your brain a well-deserved vacation. When you're always 'on,' whether it's work or digital devices, it's like your brain is running a marathon without a break.

Taking time to relax and do things you love is like hitting the refresh button. It helps you come back to work rejuvenated and ready to focus. Here's how you can incorporate relaxation into your routine:

1. **Scheduled Downtime:** Make sure to carve out time for hobbies or just to do nothing. It's like setting aside special moments for your well-being.
2. **Technology Detox:** Regularly stepping away from screens can do wonders. Imagine it as a mini digital holiday that recharges your creativity and focus.

Balancing work and life, especially when dealing with ADHD, is about creating a rhythm that works for you. It's not just about getting through the workday; it's about making sure you have the time and energy for the things that bring you joy and relaxation. So go ahead, set those boundaries, and take that time to unplug. Your mind (and work) will thank you!

Activity: Discover Your Professional Strengths and Weaknesses

This is a simple quiz to help you identify your professional strengths and weaknesses, especially in the realm of workplace relationships. After you answer these questions, I'll give you some tips on how to leverage your strengths and work on your weaknesses.

Quiz: Assessing Your Professional Strengths and Weaknesses

1. Communication: How often do you feel you effectively communicate your ideas at work?

    A) Almost always
    B) Sometimes
    C) Rarely

2. Teamwork: Do you find it easy to collaborate with others on projects?

    A) Yes, very easy
    B) It depends on the situation
    C) I struggle with this

3. Time Management: How well do you manage deadlines and work schedules?

A) I'm always on top of them

B) I manage, but it's a challenge

C) I often miss deadlines

4. Adaptability: How do you handle sudden changes or unexpected tasks at work?

A) I adapt easily

B) I can adjust, but it takes me some time

C) I find it very difficult

5. Focus: How often do you find yourself getting distracted from work tasks?

A) Rarely

B) Occasionally

C) Frequently

Scoring:

- Mostly A's: You're strong in these areas! Keep honing these skills.
- Mostly B's: You're doing well, but there's room for improvement.
- Mostly C's: These are areas where you could use some work.

Remember, everyone has their strengths and weaknesses. The key is to keep learning and growing. Use this quiz as a starting point to understand where you excel and where you could use a bit more practice. Keep at it, and you'll see improvements in no time!

As we wrap up this chapter on leveraging ADHD in the workplace, remember that managing ADHD effectively also involves honing your organizational and time management skills. These are critical tools that can turn your ADHD challenges into strengths at work. In the next chapter, we'll look into practical strategies for mastering organization and time management, essential for maximizing your professional potential with ADHD. Stay tuned for more insights and techniques that will help you thrive in your career.

Chapter 10

Mastering Organization and Time Management

D oes the clock's ticking feel like a race you're always trying to catch up with? Do you find simple tasks turning into a web of distractions in your day? If that sounds like your everyday experience, you're definitely not the only one. In this chapter, we're focusing on how you can get better at organization and time management, which is super important when you're living with ADHD.

You will learn how to tackle your tasks more effectively, manage your time like a pro, and find tools that make sense for your ADHD brain. There will be tips and tricks, real-life examples, and maybe even a few 'aha' moments. So, are you ready to take on the challenge and transform how you manage your day-to-day tasks? Let's jump in and start this journey together – it's time to make your daily to-do's a whole lot more manageable!

The Challenge of Being Organized with ADHD

Your ADHD brain has its own unique way of handling stuff, especially when it comes to organization. In your brain, there is the frontal cortex, which deals with what's called 'executive functions.' Think of your brain's frontal cortex as the control panel in a spaceship. It's where all the important stuff like decision-making, memory, and personality are managed (Huges, 2023).

In an **ADHD** brain, this control room works a bit differently. It's like the dials and switches for focus, memory, and organizing tasks are set to their own unique settings. This can make it harder for you to filter out distractions, remember all the steps of a task, or prioritize things in the order they need to happen.

So, when it feels like your brain is bouncing between a bunch of different thoughts or tasks, that's just how your executive functions are playing out. It's not that you're not trying; it's more about how your brain is processing everything. Think of it like your brain being a really creative DJ, mixing lots of tracks at once – it's a different style, but it has its own kind of rhythm and flow.

Apps for Time Management and Organization

There are some awesome apps out there designed just to make your life easier when it comes to staying organized. Think of apps like Trello, Todoist, or Evernote. They're like your personal digital assistants, helping you turn big tasks into smaller, more manageable chunks. These apps let you create lists, set priorities, and even share tasks with others if you need to. It's like having a personal organizer in your pocket that reminds you of what you need to do and helps you keep track of everything.

Using Calendar Apps for Reminders and Deadlines

Calendar apps are super handy for keeping on top of your schedule. You can use them to set reminders for appointments, deadlines, or even just daily tasks. It's like setting an alarm clock for all the different parts of your day. Most smartphones have a built-in calendar app, or you can download one that suits your style. You can set up notifications that pop up on your phone or computer so you don't forget what you need to do next. It's a great way to ensure you're always one step ahead of your schedule.

Project Management Software for Task Tracking

For bigger projects, project management software like Asana, Monday.com, or Microsoft Planner can be real game-changers. These tools are like having a command center for all your projects. You can divide each project into smaller tasks, set deadlines for each part, and track your progress. Some of these apps even let you collaborate with others, which is great if you're working in a team. They provide a visual overview of your project so you can see exactly what needs to be done and when. It's a fantastic way to keep everything organized and ensure you're making steady progress.

So, there you have it – with these apps and tools, you can turn time management and organization from a challenge into something you've got total control over. It's all about finding the right app that clicks with your style and making it a part of your daily routine. Of course, everyone is different, so here are a few tips for choosing the right organizational tools for you:

1. **Know Your Needs:** Identify the areas you struggle with most – remember appointments, keep track of tasks, or manage big projects.
2. **Look for Customization:** Opt for tools that offer customization. This way, you can tailor them to fit your specific needs and preferences.
3. **User-Friendly Interface:** Choose tools that are easy to use and understand. A cluttered or complex interface can be more of a hindrance than a help.
4. **Integration Capabilities:** Consider if the tool can integrate with other apps or devices you use. Seamless integration can make your organizational system more efficient.
5. **Trial and Error:** Don't hesitate to try out different tools to see which one works best for you. Many apps offer free trials, so take advantage of them.
6. **Seek Recommendations:** Sometimes, the best way to find a good tool is to see what works for others with ADHD. Look for recommendations in ADHD communities or forums.

By choosing the right organizational tools, you can create a system that supports your unique way of managing tasks and time. Remember, the goal is to find tools that simplify your life, not complicate it. With the right tools in hand, you can turn the challenge of organization into a manageable part of your daily routine, allowing you to focus more on what you enjoy and excel at.

The Problem of Procrastination

Let's talk about procrastination; it "is an avoidance behavior" (Sherrel, 2021). It's when you delay tasks to avoid feeling uncomfortable or stressed. But here's the thing: it's not just about being lazy. It's actually connected to how your ADHD brain works, especially regarding decision-making and staying focused.

So, why do you procrastinate? It's not because you lack willpower. It's more about how your brain sees tasks. Sometimes, it's hard for your brain to choose a boring but important task over something more fun or exciting. It's like your brain is always searching for something cool and interesting to focus on. So, even if you know you should be doing something else, your brain is drawn to things that give you instant enjoyment. The less exciting tasks often get put aside. But don't worry; it's important to understand how your ADHD brain functions.

When you procrastinate a lot, it's not just about missing deadlines; it's a whole cycle that can really mess with your stress levels and self-esteem. Imagine you've got a big report due, and you keep putting it off. The more you delay, the more that task looms over you, growing from a molehill into a mountain of stress. And when you finally rush to get it done at the last minute, the pressure is intense. Not only does this increase your stress, but it also often leads to a job that's not as good as it could have been if you'd given yourself more time.

But here's the kicker: this cycle of procrastination can make you your own worst critic. You might start thinking things like, "Why do I always do this to myself?" or "I could have done so much better if I'd started earlier." This self-blame game just adds to your stress and can really chip away at your confidence.

It's important to realize that it's not just about the hours slipping away. It's also about the impact on your emotional health. Constant stress from putting things off and then beating yourself up about it can take a toll. But luckily, recognizing this pattern is the first step towards changing it.

Once you understand what's happening, you can start working on strategies to deal with procrastination. It's about figuring out what methods help you kickstart tasks and learning to be kinder to yourself when things don't go perfectly. Remember, you're not alone in this, and finding your unique way of managing procrastination can lead to a more relaxed and confident you.

Strategies to Overcome Procrastination

Of course, you can work on overcoming your ADHD procrastination by implementing a few strategies. Some tips will work better for some than others, so try to figure out what works best for you. Here are a few tips from psychiatrist and Adult ADHD expert Scott Shapiro:

1. **Break Tasks Into Smaller Parts:** You know better than most that big tasks become overwhelming. Instead, break them into actionable microtasks. For example, instead of writing "create sales presentation" on your to-do list, break it down into research client needs, draft the presentation, and create visuals. This makes each step more manageable and less daunting.

2. **Overcome Negative Thoughts:** Replace negative thoughts with more positive, realistic ones. If you catch yourself thinking, "I can't do this," try shifting to "I'll give it a shot for 15 minutes." Changing how you talk to yourself can reduce anxiety and make starting tasks easier.

3. **Identify When You Need Help:** If you're stuck because you lack certain skills or knowledge, it's okay to seek help. Whether it's asking a colleague for advice or using available resources, getting the right support can make a big difference.

4. **Combat Perfectionism:** Perfectionism can be paralyzing. Remember, done is often better than perfect. Try to focus on progress, not perfection.

Setting realistic standards can free you from the trap of overthinking and help you start tasks more easily.

5. **Just Start:** Sometimes, the simplest advice is the most effective. Beginning a task can be the hardest part, but once you start, it often gets easier. The discomfort of starting usually fades away after a while.

6. **Communicate About Deadlines:** If you foresee missing a deadline, communicate this early and reset expectations. It's better to be upfront and realistic about what you can achieve (Shapiro, 2021).

Remember, overcoming procrastination is a process. It involves understanding your ADHD and how it influences your work habits and then applying strategies that align with your needs. By implementing these techniques, you can start to break the cycle of procrastination and find a rhythm that works for you.

Time Management Strategies

Imagine you're sitting there at the end of a long day, feeling utterly drained and frustrated. Despite your best intentions in the morning, the day slipped through your fingers. You remember the things you wanted to do, but they just didn't happen. It's not just about tasks left undone; it's the sinking feeling of being overwhelmed, the nagging sense of under-achievement, and the heavy weight of disorganization pressing down on you.

This emotional toll is precisely why mastering time management is so vital if you have ADHD. It's about more than ticking boxes off a to-do list; it's about lifting that weight off your shoulders and ending your day with a sense of peace and accomplishment.

Time Blocking

Have you ever tried time-blocking? It's like setting up a road map for your day, where you dedicate specific chunks of time to certain tasks or activities. This method is super handy, especially if you have ADHD. Why? Because it helps you prioritize and stay on track (Dr. Neff, n.d.).

Time-blocking is all about planning your day in advance, and it's especially beneficial for ADHD because it keeps you focused on one thing at a time. It prevents you from getting pulled into whatever pops up, which is often what happens when ADHD is driving the bus. So, instead of reacting to every new email or message, you carve out time for the big projects.

And here's another cool thing about time-blocking: it reduces decision fatigue and willpower drain. Making decisions all day is tiring, but with a set schedule, your calendar does the thinking for you, saving you from constant choices. Plus, just like a muscle that gets tired, willpower can run low. Time-blocking eases this strain, guiding you through your day without relying heavily on self-control. It's like having a smart assistant who plans out your day, making everything smoother and less draining.

Priorities and To-Do Lists

Let's talk about making your days smoother with some cool tricks for your to-do lists. When you've got a bunch of stuff to do, it's like having a jumbled puzzle in your head, right? Prioritizing helps sort that puzzle out. It's like picking the most important pieces first, so you're not swamped by everything at once.

Think of to-do lists as your friendly guide for the day. They line up your tasks so you can see what's up next, keeping you on track. Plus, they're great for breaking big, scary tasks into smaller, chill steps. This way, you're not staring at a mountain but climbing a bunch of little hills – way less overwhelming!

And here's a fun part: when you tick off things from your list, it feels like winning a mini-game. It's super satisfying and keeps you pumped to do more. So, by setting priorities and using to-do lists, you're not just organizing stuff; you're making your day more doable and way more fun!

While priorities and to-do lists work, setting reminders is another way to up your organization and time management game. Reminders are like having an invisible helper who's always got your back. They pop up just when you need them, saying, "Psst, don't forget this thing!" It's awesome for keeping all those little details from slipping through the cracks of your busy brain.

Setting them up is super easy – your phone, some sticky notes, or even your smart speaker can do the trick. They're like tiny assistants, always ready to remind you of what's next. This way, your brain gets to relax a bit, not having to juggle every single thing. It's like offloading your to-dos to a trusty sidekick, making your day flow smoother and keeping stress at bay.

Time Management Tips

Managing time effectively can be a bit tricky when you have ADHD, but there are some cool strategies that others have found really helpful. Here's a mix of tips that can make a big difference:

1. **Keep a Planner**: Jot down all your appointments and tasks in a planner, checking it regularly to aid memory recall.
2. **Create a To-Do List Every Day**: Start your day by making a list of tasks to tackle, keeping it realistic to avoid feeling overwhelmed.
3. **Set Phone Reminders**: Set reminders on your phone for tasks throughout the day, helping you stay focused.
4. **Prioritize Tasks**: Order your tasks by importance, using methods like numbering or color-coding for clarity.
5. **Break Tasks into 15-Minute Chunks**: Work in focused 15-minute intervals on specific tasks, taking short breaks afterward.
6. **Use a Calendar App**: Employ a digital calendar on your phone for reminders and scheduling.
7. **Arrange Essential Items**: Designate specific spots for items like keys or wallets to avoid misplacing them.

8. **Set Timers**: Use timers to gauge the duration of tasks, helping align your perception with actual time.

9. **Keep Clocks Visible**: Place clocks strategically to keep track of time and adjust your schedule accordingly.

10. **Estimate Task Time, Then Double It**: For a realistic timeframe, estimate how long a task will take and then double it.

11. **Use Sticky Notes**: Place sticky notes in strategic locations as visual cues for tasks and reminders (Hello Klarity, 2021).

Remember, what works for one person might not work for another. So, feel free to mix and match these tips to see what fits best for you. It's like making your own recipe for success!

Practical Tips for Daily Organization

Getting organized isn't just about tidying up; it's about creating a space where your mind can focus and thrive. And it's not that easy when you have ADHD, is it? So, let's dive into some handy strategies to get your daily life more organized and less like a wild treasure hunt.

Managing a Clutter-Free Space

Tackling clutter can feel like a battle, especially with an ADHD brain that often craves simplicity and order. A cluttered space can be overwhelming, muddling your thoughts just as much as it does your environment. But with some straightforward, manageable strategies, you can turn your space into a haven of organization, making it a place where focus and calm reign.

1. **Start Small**: Begin with one small area at a time, like a desk or a corner of a room. This makes the task less daunting.
2. **Use Timers**: Set a timer for short bursts of decluttering, such as 10-15 minutes. This helps to stay focused and not get overwhelmed.
3. **Regular Decluttering Sessions**: Incorporate decluttering into your routine. Even 5 minutes a day can make a big difference.
4. **Designate Spaces**: Assign specific spots for commonly used items to avoid misplacement.
5. **Declutter Digitally**: Regularly organize digital spaces like your email inbox and computer files.
6. **Donate or Discard**: Regularly review your belongings to see what you can donate to charity and what you can get rid of. That way, you avoid unnecessary accumulation.

Adopting these habits not only clears your space but also clarifies your mind, creating an environment conducive to focus and productivity. Remember, the aim isn't to achieve a perfect space but to create a functional one that resonates with your lifestyle and supports your mental well-being. These steps are less about achieving a spotless environment and more about crafting a personal space that fosters efficiency and peace.

The Benefits of the "One-Touch" Rule for Staying Organized

The "one-touch rule" is a brilliantly simple strategy to keep your world more organized and less cluttered. Imagine this: every time you pick something up, you deal with it right then and there. Picked up a bill? Pay it off. Found a letter? File it or toss it in the recycling bin. It's all about immediate action. This approach stops those piles of unsorted items from taking over your space and life.

Not only does it keep clutter in check, but it also saves you heaps of time. Think about it: when you handle things just once, you're not wasting time coming back to them over and over again. Plus, a cleaner space means a clearer mind. With fewer distractions from clutter, your focus and productivity can soar. It's like hitting two birds with one stone – you get a tidier space and a more efficient way of dealing with your daily tasks.

Strategies for Managing Paperwork and Digital Files

Do you know how paperwork and digital files can feel like they multiply overnight, especially when your mind already has a lot on its plate? It's easy to get swamped in this sea of papers and files. They pile up before you know it, making it tough to find what you need when you need it. But don't worry; there's a way to tame this chaos:

1. **Use Filing Systems**: Create a simple, easy-to-use filing system for both physical and digital documents.
2. **Go Paperless**: Where possible, opt for digital versions of documents to reduce physical clutter.
3. **Regular Clean-up**: Set aside time each week to organize and file away paperwork and digital documents.
4. **Label Clearly**: Use clear and descriptive labels for files and folders for easy retrieval.
5. **Backup Digital Files**: Regularly back up important digital files to prevent loss of data.

By setting up these systems, you're not just tidying up; you're creating a structure that makes life easier. Regular clean-ups and clear labeling mean less time hunting for documents and more time for the stuff you love. Think of it as setting up guardrails on your information highway – it keeps everything flowing smoothly so you can drive your focus where it matters most. With these steps, you're not only decluttering your space but also decluttering your mind.

How to Make a Daily Routine and Stick to It

A well-crafted routine can be a lifeline, offering stability in the whirlwind of daily life. It's like having a roadmap that guides you through the day, ensuring you don't get lost in the distractions or overwhelmed by the unexpected.

1. **Set Regular Times**: Have set times for regular activities like meals, work, and relaxation.
2. **Visual Schedules**: Use visual aids like charts or planners to keep track of your routine.
3. **Include Breaks**: Schedule short breaks to prevent burnout and maintain focus.
4. **Flexible Structure**: Be flexible enough to adjust your routine as needed but maintain a basic structure to guide your day.
5. **Review and Adjust**: Regularly review your routine and make adjustments to better suit your needs and lifestyle.

By setting up a routine that fits your ADHD brain, you're not just organizing your day; you're clearing up mental space for the cool stuff. It's about finding that sweet spot between structure and flexibility, making your days flow smoother. And remember, tweaking your routine is key to keeping it just right for you.

Now, as you start getting the hang of managing your time and space, you'll find you've got more brainpower for other big things in life. Things like keeping those impulses in check and sorting out your finances. Exciting, right? We're going to jump into all that and more in the next chapter.

Chapter 11

Managing Impulses and Financial Planning

Did you know that managing money can be extra tricky for folks with ADHD? In fact, about 65% of adults with ADHD struggle with finances because of impulse buys and budgeting blues. And get this - impulsive spending and forgetfulness can cost around £1,600 a year for 60% of us (Bautista-González, 2023). Pretty surprising, right?

In this chapter, we're going to tackle how to get a grip on those spur-of-the-moment shopping sprees and make sense of budgeting. By the end, you'll have a toolkit for keeping your spending in check and understanding why reigning in those impulses is key to better financial health. So, let's jump in and start figuring out how to make your money work for you, not against you!

Understanding Impulsive Behaviors

Have you ever found yourself at a checkout with a cart full of unplanned buys? That's impulsivity, a common trait if you have ADHD. It's about quick decisions and struggling to resist sudden urges, like blurting out thoughts or taking risks without much thought.

Impulsivity can really disrupt our daily lives, especially with spending. Imagine going to buy a few things and ending up with a cartload or making late-night online purchases that later seem unnecessary. This can throw your budget off track. The key is to become aware of these impulsive moments. Start asking, "What triggers my impulsivity? Is it a certain time, place, or emotion?" Spotting these patterns is like being a detective in your own life.

Once you're more aware, try to pause before acting on an impulse. This small break can help you think about the consequences. Set some personal rules, too, like a spending cap or a waiting period for big purchases. Tackling impulsivity isn't about being perfect; it's about steady progress. By managing these impulses, you're not only looking after your wallet but also building skills for other parts of your life.

Strategies to Control Impulsive Behaviors, Including Spending

Impulsive decision-making in adults with ADHD might look something like this: you're browsing online and see an ad for a flashy new gadget. It's sleek, high-tech, and has all the latest features. Without a second thought, you find yourself clicking 'buy now,' even though you hadn't planned to spend that money, and maybe you don't even need the gadget. It's like your brain sees something exciting and hits the go button before the part that thinks about budgets and necessities gets a chance to weigh in. This is a classic example of how impulsive decisions can happen when your ADHD brain gets caught up in the moment. But how do you manage it?

The Mindful Pause

When eyeing a big purchase, hitting the pause button is crucial. This is where a 'mindful pause' really helps. It's about taking a moment to step back and think things over (Niemiec, n.d.). Say you spot something pricey you want to buy. Instead of rushing to buy it, stop and think: Do I really need this? Is it in my budget? Is there a cheaper option?

This pause lets your brain weigh in on your impulses. It's a buffer to stop and consider your choices instead of just acting on impulse. By practicing this, you can make decisions more thoughtfully, especially with ADHD. It's about aligning your choices with your long-term goals and financial well-being rather than just going with the excitement of the moment.

Needs vs. Wants

When you're budgeting, especially with ADHD, it's super important to figure out what you really need and what you just want. Think of 'needs' as the stuff you can't live without – like your home, food, and the things that keep you healthy. 'Wants' are the extra things that are fun to have but you don't really need to get by, like eating out or the latest phone.

Sometimes, it's hard to tell the difference because we get used to having certain things. But taking the time to really think about whether something is a need or a want can help you make better choices with your money.

Tips to Tell Them Apart:

1. Look at what you're spending money on and ask yourself if you really need it or just like it.
2. Put your spending into two groups – needs and wants. This helps you see where your money's going.
3. Always make sure you've got your needs covered before you spend money on wants.
4. Every now and then, look at your spending and see if you still need what you're buying or if it's become a want.
5. It's okay to spend some money on wants; just make sure your needs are taken care of first (Pant, 2022).

When you know the difference between wants and needs, you can make a budget that works for you, keeps your spending in check, and helps you save money for the future. It's a smart way to handle your money.

Managing Impulsive Spending

Managing impulsive spending can feel like a constant battle, but with the right tools and a bit of effort, it's definitely manageable. If you're looking to get a better handle on those spur-of-the-moment purchases, here are some resources and apps that can help you out:

1. Take a 24-hour break before any big decision to think it over and sidestep impulsive spending.
2. Clarify your thoughts by recording a voice memo of your decision-making process and play it back to yourself.
3. Note down the details of what you're considering to help separate facts from emotions and make more logical decisions.
4. Consult a trusted friend or colleague for a fresh perspective when you're unsure.
5. Write out potential responses for impulsive situations to help you respond more mindfully.
6. Look deeper than just the numbers and consider all aspects of a situation to avoid biased decisions.
7. Share your tentative decision with a few trusted people and see how they react before finalizing it.
8. Keep asking 'why' to dig deeper into your initial thoughts and reach a more comprehensive decision.
9. In high-pressure moments, focus on hard facts rather than emotions to guide your actions.
10. Ponder all possible outcomes and how they match up with your final goals.

11. Push yourself to explore different perspectives or conclusions in any given situation (Forbes Coaches Council, 2017).

These strategies can greatly help you control impulsive actions, especially when it comes to money. When you use these methods, you're not only safeguarding your finances but also developing a more thoughtful and purposeful way of living.

Financial Planning and Budgeting Tips

By now, you know that your ADHD impulsivity can cause you to spend way more than planned. That's why it's important to plan your finances through budgeting. Don't worry, though. It's not as difficult as you might think. When you understand the basics, notice spending patterns, and set goals, you're on your way to managing your finances pretty darn well.

Let me ask you this: have you ever felt like your money just vanished? Like, you get paid, and then poof, it's gone? That's where a budget steps in; it helps you keep tabs on your cash. Here is a quick breakdown of how to create a budget:

1. Start by figuring out exactly what's coming in. No guesstimates!
2. Write down everything you spend, from rent to that occasional coffee treat.
3. It's like assigning jobs to your dollars.
4. Your budget should fit your real life, not an idealized version of it.

Creating a budget that works for you is all about making your money behave, meaning you're in the driver's seat. But then, what about those moments when you buy something on a whim and then wonder later, "Why did I even buy this?" I mean, you can budget to your heart's content, but if you don't track your spending, you won't know where all the money is going.

When you start tracking your spending, you might be surprised by what you find. This is a game-changer because it helps you spot those sneaky spending habits. You can do it by writing down all your purchases, looking at bank statements, or using budget tracking tools like the following:

- Simplifi by Quicken.
- Empower.
- YNAB.
- Goodbudget.
- BusyKid.
- PocketGuard.
- Honeydue.
- Monarch.
- Your Bank's App (LaPonsie, 2023).

These apps are mostly compatible with your Android or Apple smartphone, making it easy to quickly take note of your spending habits. When you have more clarity on your budget and actual spending, you can set financial goals as another way to up your budgeting game.

Having goals is like having a destination on your financial road trip. It gives you something to aim for and makes managing your money more meaningful. Think about what you want to achieve with your money. It could be anything from a dream vacation to paying off a credit card.

Finally, all of these tips are wonderful in theory, but they will only work if you actually implement them. So, to stick to a budget, here are a few final thoughts:

- **Use Budgeting Tools**: There are loads of apps that make budgeting a breeze.
- **Automate Savings**: This way, you won't be tempted to spend what you should be saving.
- **Regular Reviews**: Keep tweaking your budget so it always works for you.
- **Reward Yourself**: Got through the month without overspending? Treat yourself!

Budgeting with ADHD might feel challenging, but it's absolutely doable. It's about finding the right strategy that clicks with you. Once you get into the groove, you'll be amazed at how empowering it feels to have your finances under control. Let's tackle this together and make your financial health one less thing to worry about!

Preparing for the Future

Planning for retirement with ADHD might feel like a puzzle, but it's key to a secure future. It's like planting a tree now for shade later. Thinking ahead is crucial, especially since impulsivity in spending can disrupt long-term financial goals. There are various retirement accounts out there, each with its benefits, to help you get set for those golden years:

1. **IRAs (Individual Retirement Accounts)**: These are cool savings accounts with tax perks. You've got options like Traditional and Roth IRAs. With a Roth IRA, you pay taxes now but get tax-free money when you retire.

2. **Employer-Sponsored Plans**: Got a retirement plan at work, like a 401(k)? These are awesome for saving money. Plus, your employer might put in some extra cash, too!

3. **Automatic Contributions**: Setting up your retirement savings to happen automatically is a smart move. It's like putting your future savings on cruise control.

4. **Diverse Investments**: Mix up your investments in your retirement account. A little in stocks, some in bonds – it helps balance the risk and can give you better growth over time (Kagan, 2022).

The key to successful retirement planning, especially when you have ADHD, is to start as early as possible and make it a habit. By regularly contributing to your retirement accounts and taking advantage of compound interest over time, you can build a significant nest egg.

Remember, planning for retirement isn't just about stashing away money; it's about creating a future where financial worries don't overshadow your golden years. It's a way to balance out impulsive spending tendencies by securing your long-term financial well-being. So, let's get started on planning for a future that's as bright and secure as possible!

Estate Planning

Estate planning isn't just for the rich; it's crucial for everyone, ADHD or not. It's about deciding what happens to your stuff - money, property, and all - after you're not here. Think of it as directing your life's movie for the scenes you won't be around to see.

For those with ADHD, impulsivity might make long-term planning tough, but that's exactly why estate planning is key. It's your chance to take control and make thoughtful choices about your assets and even your healthcare. Here's how to get started:

1. **Control Over Your Assets**: Estate planning lets you decide who gets what. Without a plan, the state might make those decisions for you, and they might not align with your wishes.

2. **Protection for The Ones You Love**: It's not just about money and property; it's also about making sure the people you care about are looked after.
3. **Managing Impulsivity**: When you plan your estate, you're taking time to think through your decisions. This is a valuable practice, especially if you tend to make quick decisions without considering long-term consequences.
4. **Peace of Mind**: Knowing you've got a plan in place can give you and your loved ones peace of mind. It's like having a roadmap for the future, ensuring that your wishes are respected and followed.
5. **Financial Management**: If you struggle with managing money, estate planning can include setting up trusts or other tools to manage your assets responsibly.

Estate planning isn't just for the end of life; it's a practical way to manage your assets and ensure that your loved ones honor your wishes, no matter what happens. It's about taking control today for a more secure tomorrow.

Wills, Trusts, and Other Legal Documents

With financial planning, especially when you're navigating the waters of ADHD, there's a lot more to consider than just budgeting. It also includes things like writing a will, setting up a trust, and sorting out other legal documents play a crucial role in managing impulsivity and planning for the future.

Writing a Will

Think of a will like your final say in who gets your stuff after you're gone. It's super important because it makes sure your things - like your house, car, or savings - go exactly to the people you choose. Having a will clears up any guesswork for your family and makes sure your wishes are followed. Here's how to get started:

1. List your assets, including property, investments, and valuable possessions.
2. Choose who will inherit your assets.
3. Appoint someone who will carry out the terms of your will.
4. If you have children, decide who will take care of them.
5. Keep your will in a secure place and let your executor know where it is.
6. Do this in front of witnesses for it to be legally binding.
7. You can do this yourself, use online templates, or seek legal assistance.

Setting Up a Trust

A trust is like a special box where you put your assets (like money or property), and someone you trust manages it for people you care about. It's a smart move because it gives you more control over how your stuff is used, even after you're not around. Trusts can also help save on taxes and protect your assets. Get started with these steps:

1. Determine what you want the trust to achieve (e.g., care for a family member and manage assets).
2. Decide between a living trust (active during your lifetime) or a testamentary trust (activated after death).
3. Choose who will manage the trust.
4. Clearly state how the assets should be managed and distributed.
5. Use legal services or online resources to draft the document.
6. Sign the document in front of a notary to make it official.
7. Transfer assets into the trust.

Other Important Legal Documents

Besides wills and trusts, there are other big-deal documents like healthcare directives and financial power of attorney. These are super important because they lay out your choices about your health care and money if someday you can't make those calls yourself. They help your family know exactly what you want, making tough times a little easier. Consider the following steps:

1. Outline your wishes for medical care if you're unable to make decisions yourself.
2. Have a designated person to take care of you're finances when you are unable.

3. Ensure your retirement accounts and insurance policies have named beneficiaries.
4. Provide a personal message to your beneficiaries or executor.

Remember, these steps we're talking about are really important. Keep in mind that the process might be a bit different for everyone, depending on their own situation and the laws in their area. It's always a good idea to reach out to a legal professional, especially if you have a more complex estate or specific wishes.

By going through these steps, you're not only getting your assets organized, but you're also making things easier for your loved ones. It's like giving them a clear roadmap and peace of mind. And if you happen to have ADHD, this kind of planning can be even more empowering. It helps balance out any impulsive tendencies and ensures that your wishes are respected and followed.

Activity: Creating Your Simple Budget

Let's get hands-on and create a simple budget. This will help you understand where your money is going and how you can manage it better. Here's a straightforward template to guide you:

1. **Calculate Your Income**: Start by jotting down your monthly income.
2. **List Essential Expenses**: Next, list out your essential expenses.
3. **Set Financial Goals**: Now, think about your financial goals.
4. **Allocate Money to Goals**: Decide how much money you want to put towards each goal every month.
5. **Track Non-Essential Spending**: Keep an eye on your non-essential spending.
6. **Review and Adjust**: At the end of each month, review your budget. Did you stick to your goals? Where did you overspend?

Remember, a budget is not about restricting yourself; it's about empowering you to make informed decisions about your money. So start simple and remain consistent. With time, you'll find it easier to manage your finances and work towards your goals.

Now that you've got a grip on managing your impulses and finances, we're ready to dive into another exciting area. In Chapter 12, we'll explore how gaining control over another aspect of life can bring even more peace and balance. We're talking about balancing emotions through mindfulness and spirituality.

It's all about finding inner calm and a sense of center, something that can be truly transformative. So, let's turn the page and delve into the world of mindfulness and spirituality, and discover how these practices can enhance your life in ways you might not have imagined!

Chapter 12

Balancing Emotions Through Mindfulness and Spirituality

Meet Rebecca, a 41-year-old who embraced mindfulness to navigate her ADHD journey. Initially, meditation was a struggle, but guided apps like Headspace gradually eased her into it. On tougher days, Rebecca found solace in yoga, using it to connect her breath with movement and to stay grounded in the present moment. Even simple acts like focusing on the shower's sensations became opportunities for mindfulness.

Recently diagnosed with ADHD, she found that mindfulness significantly eased her anxiety. It allowed her to step back and view her emotions more objectively, offering a sense of calm amidst the chaos of her thoughts.

Rebecca's story, like many others, demonstrates the profound impact mindfulness and spirituality can have on managing ADHD. It's a journey of turning inward, finding peace in small moments, and learning to approach life with a mindful perspective.

Digging Deeper into Mindfulness

Mindfulness is all about staying aware of the here and now without judging it as good or bad. It's like a mental exercise that helps you focus on the present moment instead of thinking about the past or future. This practice, rooted in Buddhist meditation, has become popular in recent years, especially thanks to Jon Kabat-Zinn and his program called Mindfulness-Based Stress Reduction (MBSR) (Kabat-Zinn, 2019). MBSR has been shown to have many health benefits, and we'll dive deeper into how it can help you manage your emotions in the next sections.

To deepen your level of mindfulness, here are a few techniques you can try. They're based on the work of psychiatrist and adult ADHD and mindfulness-based therapy expert Dr. Zylowska:

Mindful labeling means acknowledging and naming your thoughts, emotions, and bodily reactions without being critical. Here's how to do it:

- Find a quiet, comfy spot.
- Take a few deep breaths to relax.
- Pay attention to your thoughts and feelings.
- Either say or think about what you're experiencing, like, "I feel anxious, and my heart is racing."
- Practice this for 5-10 minutes daily.

Refocus Your Attention means redirecting your focus away from worries and toward the present moment. Here's how to do it:

1. Practice deep breathing exercises: Inhale deeply for a count of four, pause, exhale for a count of four, and pause again. Keep your focus on the sensation of your breath.
2. Try imagery: Visualize calm energy entering with each inhale and stress leaving with each exhale.
3. Engage in informal activities: Take a walk in nature, listen to music, write down your thoughts, or do yoga.
4. Continue refocusing your attention on your chosen activity.

Return to the Situation involves revisiting the triggering situation to understand the underlying anxiety. To do it, try this:

1. After practicing mindfulness, return to the situation that caused anxiety.
2. Experience the feelings without getting overwhelmed.
3. Ask questions like "What caused my worry?" "Why does this situation worry me?" "Am I engaging in unhelpful thinking patterns?" or "Can I address the worry or learn to tolerate uncertainty?"
4. Reflect on the insights gained.

Learn Self-Coaching involves developing a supportive inner voice to navigate challenges. Here's how to do it:

1. Cultivate an inner voice that encourages. It improves compassion by checking in on your feelings, helps you pace yourself, holds you accountable for ADHD challenges, and keeps you connected to your core values. It's like having a supportive friend in your head, guiding you through the ups and downs of life with ADHD.
2. Use your inner coach to guide you through difficulties and decision-making.

Practicing mindfulness can be tricky, especially if you're super busy or easily distracted. But here's how to tackle it: Start small and gradually make it longer. Use reminders to keep you on track, and find a quiet spot. If your mind wanders, don't worry; just bring it back gently. You can use apps or guided sessions to help. The most important thing is to keep at it, even if it's just for a short time each day. You'll still see the benefits!

Spiritual Practices for Emotional Balance

Spiritual practices like prayer, meditation, Bible study, serving others, worship, and sharing one's faith can be great ways to find emotional balance. But for folks with ADHD, these practices can sometimes be a bit tricky. Let's take a look at a few practices:

1. **Prayer:** Finding the right time to pray regularly can be a challenge, and remembering what you want to pray about can be tough, too. Keeping a prayer journal or using prayer logs can be super helpful. Also, finding a quiet spot to pray can be a good idea because it's easier to hear what God might be saying when things are calm.

2. **Bible Study:** Reading the Bible cover to cover might be a big ask for someone with ADHD. It's totally okay to focus on the most important parts that speak to you. Using highlighters can make it more engaging.

3. **Meditation:** Sitting still and thinking quietly can be a bit hard, especially if your mind tends to wander. Short, guided meditations that give clear directions can work better.

4. **Service:** Doing chores might not be the most exciting thing, but doing something meaningful that matches your interests and skills can be amazing. Like helping build houses for single moms or working on projects that make a difference.

5. **Worship:** Getting involved in worship activities rather than just watching can be more enjoyable. You might even end up performing on stage, like some kids who love it!

6. **Evangelism:** Sometimes, having a bit of impulsivity can be a plus, especially when sharing your faith with others. Instead of overthinking, you might just go for it (Grcevich, 2010).

Remember, there's no one-size-fits-all. As long as you get something that works for you, you'll be on your way to proper emotional balance. When you have a strong sense of spirituality, you tend to feel more at peace, hopeful, and confident. It's like having a trusted friend inside you, helping you make sense of things when life gets tough and giving you the strength to bounce back when you're not feeling your best.

But there's a word of caution, too. Just like in life, there can be people who take advantage of those who are feeling vulnerable. So, it's essential to stay grounded in your spirituality and not let anyone exploit your emotions. Remember, your spiritual journey is there to uplift you and make you stronger, not to bring you down.

Incorporating spirituality into your daily life, especially when dealing with ADHD, can be a powerful source of strength and balance. Start by setting aside a few minutes each day for quiet reflection or meditation. Find a comfortable and quiet space where you can connect with your spiritual beliefs, whether through prayer, mindfulness, or simply taking deep breaths to center yourself.

Consider joining a spiritual community or group where there are other like-minded people you can share your journey with. Find and take part in spiritual practices that resonate with you, whether it's reading spiritual texts, practicing gratitude, or participating in acts of kindness.

Activity: A Guided Mindfulness Exercise

As we wrap up this chapter, I've set a simple yet powerful 5-minute breathing exercise. This will be a small step into the world of mindfulness, helping you connect with the present moment. Here's what to do:

1. **Find a Quiet Space**: Choose a comfortable and quiet spot where you won't be disturbed.
2. **Set a Timer**: Set a timer for 5 minutes. This will help you stay focused on the exercise without worrying about the time.
3. **Adopt a Comfortable Position**: Sit or lie down in a comfortable position. You can sit on a chair with your feet on the ground or on the floor with your legs crossed.
4. **Close Your Eyes**: Gently close your eyes. This helps minimize distractions and focus inward.
5. **Focus on Your Breath**: Pay attention to your breathing. Notice the sensation of air flowing into your nose, fill your chest and belly, and flow out of your nose again.
6. **Breathe Naturally**: Don't try to control your breath. Just breathe naturally and observe.
7. **Return to Your Breath**: Your mind will likely wander. That's okay. Whenever you find that your thoughts are drifting, bring your focus back to your breathing without judgment.

8. **Be Kind to Yourself**: Remember, it's normal for the mind to wander. Be gentle with yourself when it happens.

After the timer goes off, take a moment to notice how you feel. Slowly open your eyes and reacquaint yourself with your surroundings. As you work on balancing your emotions through mindfulness and spirituality, it's important to recognize that this journey not only benefits you but also has a positive impact on your family and loved ones. The newfound emotional balance and clarity you discover will allow you to navigate various aspects of life more effectively.

In the next chapter, we'll delve into the joys and challenges of parenting when you have ADHD. Parenthood brings unique experiences and responsibilities, and understanding how to manage them in the context of ADHD can lead to more harmonious family dynamics.

Chapter 13

Parenting with ADHD

L et me introduce you to Lily. She is a parent with ADHD who has to juggle motherhood alongside her symptoms. Her day is packed with a flurry of activities: meetings at work, household tasks, and keeping up with personal commitments. Amidst this hectic schedule, there's something crucial Lily needs to remember: her child's school play. But as the day unfolds with one task leading to another, the evening sneaks up on her. That's when her child comes home, a look of disappointment in their eyes. "Mom, you forgot my play," they say softly. Lily's heart sinks. Despite all the reminders and lists, the play had slipped through the cracks.

This scenario isn't just about a missed event. It's a snapshot of the life of a parent grappling with ADHD. It illustrates the struggle of balancing parenting responsibilities while managing ADHD symptoms. In this chapter, we'll go into the world of parenting with ADHD. We'll discuss actionable strategies for managing ADHD symptoms and becoming a more effective, empathetic parent. By the end of this chapter, you'll have practical tools to enhance your family dynamics and smooth out the parenting journey.

How Being a Parent with ADHD Affects Family Dynamics

Parenting with ADHD is like going on a treasure hunt without a map – it's unpredictable but full of surprises! It definitely affects your family dynamics in a few interesting ways. For example, forgetfulness becomes a familiar companion in your daily adventures. Have you ever put cereal in the fridge and milk in the cupboard? It adds a quirky twist to family life, like when school lunches turn into mystery boxes because you mixed up the snack packs.

And then there's impulsivity – your wildcard trait. Spontaneous pillow forts in the living room? Check. These impromptu moments bring laughter but can also shake up your routines a bit. But here's the real treasure: these ADHD traits sprinkle extra creativity into your family life. Sure, you might occasionally stray from the conventional path, but you're a champion at crafting memorable experiences and thinking outside the box.

Having ADHD doesn't make you a bad or irresponsible parent. It's just a different way of experiencing the world. ADHD in adults often means dealing with brain fog, poor memory, and getting easily distracted. These challenges can affect how you manage family life, from keeping track of appointments to maintaining emotional availability for your kids.

The key is to show yourself some compassion. By breaking out of the guilt cycle, you'll find the motivation to make positive changes. It's about understanding how ADHD affects your parenting and learning to navigate its impact.

For instance, ADHD can make emotional regulation tough. You might find it hard to consistently provide warmth and structure or to be fully present for your kids. Developing strategies to better manage your emotions and stress can help. Simple practices like self-care, pausing before reacting, and stepping away when overwhelmed can make a big difference.

Communication is another tricky area. You might drift off during conversations or unintentionally interrupt your kids, leaving them feeling unheard. Working on active listening and being present at the moment can help build stronger connections with your children.

Then there's organization and time management – not exactly ADHD's strong suits. This can lead to missed events, clutter, and inconsistent routines. But remember, perfection isn't the goal; progress is. Every small step towards better organization counts.

And if you're a mom with ADHD, you might face additional challenges. Women's ADHD symptoms often go undiagnosed, and they're more likely to deal with co-occurring anxiety or depression. With the added pressure of household and childcare responsibilities, it's vital to seek support and prioritize your well-being.

But if you still feel a bit overwhelmed, let's look at some real-life stories of parents with ADHD and how they affect their family dynamics:

1. **Parent 1:** "I have ADHD and two young kids. Managing daily activities and avoiding burnout is a constant struggle. Every day is different and unpredictable. While my children are always cared for and loved, I often struggle to take care of myself."

2. **Parent 2:** "Both my child and I likely have ADHD. We've found that getting outside every day, keeping meals simple, and accepting our somewhat chaotic morning routine helps. We also use warnings before activity changes and enforce quiet time when needed. Understanding each other's ADHD behaviors offers insights into managing our daily lives."

3. **Parent 3:** "I'm a parent with ADHD, and my son has ADHD and ASD. Coping can be challenging. Lists and alarms help with scheduling, but frequent burnout is an issue. Watching him requires constant vigilance, which can be draining" (*Parents with ADHD?*, 2022).

Remember, like in an airplane safety briefing, you need to put on your oxygen mask first before helping others. By taking care of your needs and seeking professional help, you'll be in a much stronger position to support and raise your kids.

Strategies for Effective Parenting

When it comes to parenting with ADHD, the conventional playbook might not always be the best fit. Traditional parenting tips, while well-intentioned, often don't take into account the unique challenges and strengths that come with ADHD. And trying to apply those tips can leave ADHD parents feeling more frustrated than supported.

It's important to recognize that ADHD brains are wired differently, and that's okay! What works for one family might not work for another, especially when ADHD is part of the equation. That's why it's best to find strategies that align with your unique strengths and challenges as an ADHD parent. Let's explore some tips that can help you thrive in your parenting journey:

1. **Make ADHD Management a Priority:** It's crucial to keep your ADHD well-managed. This might involve medication, behavioral therapy, or a combination of both. Effective management can help you maintain your daily routines, manage your emotional reactions, and pay better attention to your kids' positive behaviors.

2. **Schedule Quality Time:** With ADHD, it's easy to get sidetracked and miss out on spending focused time with your children. Plan specific times each day for your kids. Write these sessions in your planner or set phone reminders to help you stay committed.

3. **Utilize Timers:** Use timers to remind yourself to check in on your kids at regular intervals. This not only helps keep them safe but also ensures that you're giving them the attention they need, especially if they also have ADHD.

4. **Consistency is Key:** ADHD can lead to impulsive responses, which can be confusing for kids. Create a list of family rules and corresponding consequences. Display this list prominently and refer to it to maintain consistency in your responses.

5. **Embrace Time-Outs (for You!):** When you're feeling overwhelmed, it's important to take a break. Plan regular alone time for activities you enjoy. This helps regulate your emotions and prevents overreactions.

6. **Share Responsibilities:** Recognize your strengths and delegate tasks that are challenging for you. If time management isn't your forte, let someone else handle time-sensitive tasks. Conversely, take on responsibilities that are more flexible, like household chores.

7. **Communicate with Your Therapist:** Discuss your parenting strengths and challenges with your therapist. They can tailor a treatment plan to help you address specific areas where you need support, such as maintaining focus on parenting tasks.

8. **Continuous Learning:** If you or your children have ADHD, consider enrolling in behavioral parenting training (BPT). These classes teach effective parenting techniques tailored to ADHD challenges.

Extended BPT sessions can be particularly beneficial for parents with ADHD, helping to make these new skills second nature (McMillen, 2022).

By adapting these strategies to fit your unique situation, you can navigate the challenges of parenting with ADHD more effectively. Remember, the goal isn't perfection but progress. Celebrate the small victories and be kind to yourself on this journey. That includes embracing self-care and seeking support when needed.

1. **Self-Care is Your Secret Weapon:** Remember, doing things you enjoy, like a hobby or just chilling, isn't selfish. It's charging your batteries to be the best parent you can be.
2. **Asking for Help is Cool:** Whether it's family, friends, or your partner, it's okay to ask for a hand. Sharing chores or just talking can really help.
3. **Find People Who Get It:** Support groups are awesome for meeting other parents with ADHD. You can swap stories and tips.
4. **Pros Can Help Too:** If things are tough, talking to a therapist can really help. They're like guides in your parenting journey.

And hey, all this stuff about taking care of yourself and getting help? It's not just for parenting. It's the same deal when it comes to handling money, work, and relationships. Sometimes, getting advice from someone who gets it – like a financial advisor or a career coach – can really help.

Building Emotional Resilience in Your Kids

When it comes to raising kids, especially if you're a parent with ADHD, one of the greatest gifts you can give them is emotional resilience. Kids of parents with ADHD might need extra emotional support because they often experience more unpredictability in their daily lives. This can sometimes make them feel insecure or misunderstood. But don't worry; there are plenty of ways to boost their resilience and emotional intelligence.

Tips for Teaching Resilience and Emotional Intelligence

Resilience is bouncing back from challenges, while emotional intelligence involves understanding and managing emotions, both yours and others. Here's how you can cultivate both in your children:

1. **Invite Open Communication:** Create a safe space where your kids feel comfortable sharing their feelings. Ask them about their day, their worries, and their victories. Listen actively and validate their emotions.

2. **Problem-Solving Skills:** Teach them to see challenges as opportunities to learn. Guide them through problem-solving steps: understanding the problem, brainstorming solutions, and trying them out. This approach helps them feel more in control and capable.

3. **Positive Relationships:** Encourage your kids to build strong relationships with family members, friends, and teachers. These connections provide them with a support network and a sense of belonging.

4. **Develop Coping Skills:** Teach your kids healthy ways to deal with stress and disappointment. This could be through deep breathing, taking a walk, or drawing. Coping skills are crucial for emotional well-being.

5. **Promote a Growth Mindset:** Help them understand that they can develop skills and intelligence with effort. Praise their efforts and persistence rather than just the outcome. This mindset encourages them to embrace learning and growth.

6. **Set Realistic Goals:** Teach your children to set goals that are both realistic and achievable. Then, teach them to break them down into smaller steps. This helps them experience success and builds their confidence.

7. **Encourage Independence:** Give your kids age-appropriate responsibilities. This could be as simple as picking out their clothes or helping with chores. It fosters independence and a sense of accomplishment.

Modeling Emotional Resilience

As a parent with ADHD, you might struggle with emotional regulation yourself. However, you can still model resilience for your kids. When you face challenges, talk openly about them and how you're dealing with them. Let your kids see you managing your emotions and stress in healthy ways. This teaches them that it's okay to have difficult emotions and that there are constructive ways to handle them.

Building Skills Together

Finally, remember that teaching your kids resilience and emotional intelligence is not just beneficial for them; it's also a way to improve your own emotional well-being. As you guide your kids, you reinforce these skills in yourself. It's a journey you take together, growing and learning as a family.

Building emotional resilience in your children equips them to go through life's ups and downs with confidence. It's a process, but with patience, love, and a bit of creativity, you can help your kids become emotionally strong and resilient.

Activity: Strengthening Family Bonds

As we wrap up this chapter on parenting with ADHD, here's a meaningful activity to bring you closer to your family. When you spend quality time together, it helps create stronger bonds and understanding within your family. Below is a checklist of activities that can help you achieve just that:

1. **Family Game Night:** Schedule a weekly time when everyone gathers to play board games, card games, or interactive video games.
2. **Cooking Together:** Pick a day to cook a meal together. Let each family member choose a dish or an ingredient to contribute.
3. **Nature Walks:** Plan a weekly walk in a nearby park or nature trail. Use this time to talk, explore, and enjoy the outdoors together.
4. **Movie Nights:** Have a weekly movie night where a different family member gets to pick the movie. Don't forget the popcorn!
5. **Storytelling Time:** Share stories from your childhood, listen to your children's stories, or read a book together. This can be a great bedtime ritual.
6. **Arts and Crafts:** Set aside time for a family arts and crafts session. This can be as simple as drawing, painting, or working on a DIY project together.
7. **Family Meetings:** Hold a regular family meeting to discuss any upcoming events, any concerns, or simply to check in with each other.
8. **Volunteer as a Family:** Choose a local charity or community event where you can volunteer together.
9. **Plan a Day Trip:** Once a month, plan a day trip to explore a new place or revisit a favorite spot.
10. **Gratitude Jar:** Create a family gratitude jar where everyone can drop notes about what they are thankful for. Read them together at the end of the month.

Remember, it's not about how much time you spend together, but the quality of that time. These activities are building blocks for a lifetime of love and understanding. Choose activities that resonate with your family and start creating those special memories today.

As we close this chapter on parenting with ADHD, it's important to recognize that ADHD doesn't exist in isolation. Many factors, including gender and various social elements, influence it. These aspects shape how ADHD is experienced and managed in day-to-day life. In the upcoming chapter, we're going to look at how gender and other social factors play a crucial role in the ADHD experience. Each person's journey with ADHD is unique and influenced by their environment, societal expectations, and personal identities. Understanding these nuances means you're developing a more holistic approach to managing ADHD.

Chapter 14

ADHD, Gender, and Intersectionality

B efore we start with this chapter, I'd like to introduce you to Callum and Jordan. Callum is always on the move, interrupts meetings, and seems to juggle a million tasks at once; Jordan misses deadlines, gets lost in details, and often seems to drift away during discussions. Both face challenges in their professional lives, but while Callum's hyperactive behaviors draw immediate attention, Jordan's quieter, inattentive struggles go unnoticed. It just goes to show how ADHD is far from a 'one size fits all' condition, especially when it comes to adults.

ADHD in adulthood is a complex interplay of factors, including gender, cultural background, and social contexts. For men, it often manifests in more observable hyperactive and impulsive behaviors. Women, on the other hand, might experience ADHD with subtler, inattentive symptoms, which can be easily overlooked or misinterpreted.

In this chapter, we will look at the multifaceted world of adult ADHD, exploring how it intersects with gender and other identity aspects. It's a journey that reveals the diverse experiences of those living with ADHD, highlighting the importance of understanding these differences for more effective recognition, support, and treatment.

ADHD Across Genders

You probably know how sometimes we think everyone with ADHD is kind of the same, right? Well, it turns out it's way more complicated than that, especially when we talk about how it shows up in men, women, and non-binary folks. Let's dive into this and bust some myths along the way.

It might seem like ADHD is more common in guys, but there's a lot more to the story. Women often don't get diagnosed as much because their ADHD symptoms can be more subtle, not the big, loud ones we usually hear about. Instead of being hyperactive, they might be lost in thought or forget things easily.

For a lot of men, ADHD can look like being all over the place, like they just can't sit still. However, women with ADHD might experience things differently. It's often what's going on in their minds, such as overthinking or feeling their emotions very intensely, that signals ADHD.

Usually, ADHD symptoms show up by the time someone is 12 years old, but it can be different for boys and girls. Boys often show symptoms earlier, while girls might not show or even notice their symptoms until they're older, sometimes not until they're adults.

Getting diagnosed with ADHD in adulthood, especially for women, can be a complex process. It's easy to mistake ADHD for stress or anxiety. These days, more women in their 30s and 40s are being diagnosed with ADHD, which could be partly due to the recent lifestyle changes, like those brought on by the pandemic, which has disrupted usual routines and brought underlying issues to the surface (Mandriota, 2022).

Alright, let's clear up some things about ADHD, especially when it comes to adults. You might have heard that ADHD is mostly a guy thing. Well, that's not really true. And there's this idea that men with ADHD are always super hyper while women are just daydreamers. But honestly, ADHD is different for everyone and doesn't just stick to these stereotypes.

Now, when we talk about treating ADHD, it's a bit different for men and women. For guys, it's often about figuring out how to deal with all that extra energy they have. They need to find ways to use it well without going overboard. For women, it's more about getting a grip on all those racing thoughts and trying to keep things organized. Plus, women have to deal with changes in their bodies, like during their monthly cycle or menopause, which can really mess with their ADHD. It's all about finding the right balance and what works best for each person.

When it comes to non-binary pals, the ADHD story can vary a lot. Their experiences are super individual and might not match the typical ADHD stories we hear. What they need is support that gets both their gender and their ADHD.

So, ADHD isn't the same for everyone. It changes from person to person, and gender plays a big part in that. If you think you might have ADHD and it's mixed up with your gender experiences, having a chat with a therapist could be a game-changer. The main thing? It's all about understanding yourself better and making life smoother, no matter who you are.

Intersectionality and ADHD

Ever wondered how different aspects of who you are, like your race, background, or who you love, interact with ADHD? That's what we call intersectionality. It's about understanding how all these pieces come together to shape your experience with ADHD. It goes beyond just ADHD by itself; it's about how it connects with all the other parts of your life.

Think about it this way: where you come from, and your cultural background can have a big impact on how you handle ADHD. It's a bit like how your surroundings shape your experiences. Let's say you grew up in a neighborhood where many families struggle financially. In such areas, it can be tough to find the right help and support for ADHD. The resources may not be as available, and that can make managing ADHD more challenging.

Now, picture living in a community where talking about mental health isn't common. Seeking help for ADHD might feel like trying to climb a steep hill. It's not that the help isn't there; it's just that it's not talked about openly. And then there are individuals in LGBTQ+ communities. Their experience of ADHD can be even more unique. Finding support that understands their specific challenges can be like looking for a needle in a haystack.

Navigating the Healthcare System

Finding suitable ADHD support when you have multiple aspects of your identity can be like solving a puzzle. The key is to connect with healthcare professionals who truly understand you – not just your ADHD but also the diverse facets of your life. You need someone who listens attentively and recognizes the full scope of your identity.

Although I've mentioned her before, let's look at Simone Biles again. She is a remarkable gymnast who doesn't just manage ADHD but she's also a Black woman, which adds another dimension and layer of complexity to her story. When she shared her ADHD diagnosis and the need for medication, it garnered significant attention, but not all of it was positive. This illustrates how being in the spotlight with ADHD becomes more intricate when intersecting factors like race and gender are involved.

To sum it up, when we discuss ADHD and intersectionality, we're acknowledging its complexity. The various facets of your identity mold your experience with ADHD. Understanding this complexity promotes better mutual understanding and ensures that everyone receives the support they require.

Activity: Reflection Time

Alright, you've just finished this chapter about ADHD, gender, and all that intersects with them. Now, it's cool to take a little break and think about what you've picked up. This is like a mini-adventure into your own thoughts. Grab a piece of paper, or just mull over these questions in your head:

1. **Did Anything Surprise You?** Think about how you saw ADHD before and how you see it now. Did you learn something new or unexpected?
2. **Does It Remind You of Anyone?** Maybe you or someone you know has ADHD. Does this chapter make you think differently about their experiences?
3. **Why's This Important?** How do you think understanding ADHD in different people can help us all be more supportive and understanding?
4. **What Will You Remember?** Pick one or two things from the chapter that really stuck with you. How can you use these in your day-to-day life?
5. **Walking in Their Shoes:** How might your new knowledge about ADHD change the way you talk to or think about others with ADHD?

This isn't just about remembering stuff from the chapter; it's about making it part of how you think and act. By pondering these questions, you're helping yourself be more aware and kind towards people with ADHD.

There's one big idea that really shines through this chapter: having a strong support network is like having a superpower when it comes to managing ADHD. This becomes even more important when we think about all the stuff we've talked about – how ADHD is different for everyone and how things like gender and background can change the way it shows up in people's lives.

Now, let's get ready to dive into our next chapter. Here, we're going to explore how to build and strengthen that crucial support network. It's all about finding the right people who get it, who understand the twists and turns of your ADHD journey, and who can be there for you in just the right ways. This chapter is going to be a roadmap to help you find and nurture those key relationships that make all the difference.

Chapter 15

Building Your ADHD Support Network

"Alone, you can do so little; together, you can do so much."

— *Helen Keller*

In the world of ADHD, these words should remind you that your journey with ADHD is not one you need to embark on alone. It is a complex, multifaceted condition, and navigating its challenges is easier when you have a support network by your side. Imagine a world where people with ADHD are not isolated but connected, where the power of community transforms lives. And as grand as it may seem, it's not difficult to become part of that world. That's where the profound impact of building your ADHD support network comes in. It's a journey that promises understanding, empathy, and the strength to thrive.

Why Community Matters

Social support means having people in your corner who care about you and can help in different ways. Back in 1905, a doctor named Joseph Pratt gathered a group of people with tuberculosis and found that support from others improved their health (Primary Health Care-The Project, 2017). Today, we know that social support reduces stress, boosts your immune system, and can even save lives.

Having a strong social network, whether it's friends, family, or support groups, gives you a sense of belonging and security. When you have ADHD, this support can make a massive difference in how you navigate the challenges in your life. It's about thriving with the help of those who care about you. And while support, in general, is important for anyone, whether they have ADHD or not, the right type of support is what makes the difference. Social support comes in various forms, each offering unique benefits.

1. **Emotional Support**: Sometimes, all you need is someone who understands and listens. Emotional support involves comforting gestures like hugs, empathetic listening, and words of comfort. It lets you know you're not alone in your struggles.
2. **Esteem Support**: This type of support boosts your confidence. It can be as simple as compliments, affirmations, or reminding you of your strengths. When someone believes in you, it helps you believe in yourself.

3. **Informational Support**: Sometimes, you need guidance and advice. Informational support provides facts and solutions. It can include sharing knowledge, offering resources, or giving step-by-step instructions to tackle challenges.

4. **Tangible Support**: This is about practical help. It includes actions like lending money, offering a ride, doing chores, or providing childcare. Tangible support takes the load off your shoulders so you can focus on addressing your ADHD (Scott, 2010).

Different types of support work differently for each person and situation. So, it's a good idea to recognize your needs and seek the right type of support. While the wrong support can be counterproductive, going at it alone isn't good either. Without a supportive community, you may face several challenges:

1. **Isolation**: ADHD can sometimes make you feel isolated or misunderstood. Without a community, you might struggle to connect with others who share similar experiences.

2. **Lack of Understanding**: Those who haven't experienced ADHD firsthand may not fully understand the daily challenges it presents. And that can lead to frustration and miscommunication between neurotypical and neurodivergent people.

3. **Limited Resources**: Building a support network provides access to valuable resources, information, and coping strategies that you might miss out on when going alone.

4. **Increased Stress**: The stress of managing ADHD on your own can be overwhelming. Luckily, having a supportive community can offer emotional and practical help, reducing the burden.
5. **Missed Opportunities**: Without a community, you might miss out on opportunities for personal growth, learning, and support.

This is why community matters. A supportive network of understanding friends, family, or peers can make a world of difference in your ADHD journey. It gives you a sense of belonging, reduces isolation, and offers a safety net when things get challenging.

Finding Your Tribe: ADHD Groups and Online Forums

Navigating life with ADHD is made easier when you have a community that truly understands your experiences. Finding an ADHD support group can provide you with valuable connections, advice, and a sense of belonging. Whether you prefer in-person meetings or online forums, here's how to find your tribe:

In today's digital age, online forums like Reddit's r/ADHD provide a crucial platform for adults with ADHD. These spaces offer a sense of community, allowing individuals to share experiences, seek advice, and connect with diverse perspectives. The anonymity of online platforms can be comforting for those hesitant to discuss ADHD openly.

- **Reddit**: Platforms like r/ADHD on Reddit are great for anonymous discussions and seeking advice. Remember to respect community guidelines, and keep in mind that advice from non-professionals should be taken with caution.
- **Facebook Groups**: There are numerous ADHD-related Facebook groups with diverse communities. Search for groups that align with your interests, whether it's adult ADHD, parenting with ADHD, or specific topics like medication management.
- **Twitter and Instagram**: Follow ADHD advocates, psychologists, and organizations on social media for informative content and connections. When you engage in conversations with like-minded individuals, it can be enlightening and stimulating.

Online platforms are good ways to seek support, but local support groups remain vital. They provide a safe space to meet in person or virtually, fostering a sense of belonging and meaningful connections. These groups remind us of the importance of real-life human connections in navigating ADHD's complexities.

- **Check Local Listings**: Search online or in community listings for local ADHD support groups. These may meet in person or virtually, depending on your location.
- **Meetup.com**: Meetup is a platform that helps people find and build local communities. You can

often find ADHD support groups or social meetups in your area.

- **University or Healthcare Centers**: Contact nearby universities or healthcare centers, as they may host ADHD support groups or have information on local resources.

What to Look for in a Support Group

When choosing an ADHD support group, consider the following factors:

- **Focus**: Some groups may concentrate on specific aspects of ADHD, such as coping strategies, medication management, or emotional well-being. Choose a group that aligns with your needs.
- **Facilitator Qualifications**: If a facilitator leads the group, inquire about their qualifications or background in ADHD-related fields.
- **Size and Structure**: Determine if you prefer a small, intimate group or a larger, more diverse one. Some groups may follow structured formats, while others offer more casual discussions.
- **Inclusivity**: Look for groups that are inclusive and respectful of diverse backgrounds, genders, and experiences.
- **Meeting Frequency**: Consider your availability and how often you'd like to participate. Some groups meet weekly, biweekly, or monthly.

- **Online Safety**: In online forums, prioritize your privacy and safety. Use pseudonyms if desired, and avoid sharing personal information.

Don't be discouraged if the first group you join doesn't feel like the right fit. Finding your tribe may take some trial and error. Keep exploring different groups until you discover one where you feel comfortable sharing and learning.

Remember that support groups are there to provide encouragement, understanding, and shared wisdom. By actively participating, you can enhance your ADHD journey and build lasting connections with others who truly "get it."

Blank page is for activity.

Activity: Mapping Your ADHD Support Network

Having a strong support network is important. It means recognizing the people who are already part of your network, figuring out where there are gaps, and finding ways to fill those gaps to meet your specific needs. Here's a simple activity that can help you map out your own personalized network:

1. Create a Visual Map: Begin by drawing a circle in the center labeled "Me." Extend lines outward to represent your current support network.
2. Assess Strength: Take a moment to evaluate the strength of each connection within your network. Use a scale from 1 to 5, considering factors like trust, understanding, and reliability.

3. Identify Gaps: As you assess your network, identify any areas where you may be lacking sufficient support or understanding. Mark these gaps on your map.

4. Set Actionable Steps: Brainstorm actionable steps you can take to strengthen the aspects of your support network that require improvement.

5. Prioritize Actions: Determine which steps hold the most significance for you. When you do, think about the immediate and long-term benefits of each action and prioritize accordingly.

6. Create a Support Plan: Write down your actionable steps and create a clear timeline for when you intend to take each one. Be specific about who you will contact, what you will say, and how you plan to follow through.

7. Take the First Step: Begin implementing your plan by taking the first step you've outlined.

8. Track Progress: Revisit your support network map and update it as your connections strengthen.

This activity will help you visualize your support network, identify areas for improvement, and take actionable steps toward building a stronger and more understanding community around you. Not only will you feel less alone, but you'll have people around you who understand what you're going through.

As you close the chapter on building your ADHD support network, remember that you're never alone on this journey. In the conclusion, we'll bring everything together and give you actionable steps to make the most of your life, ADHD and all.

A Chance to Help

As you shed many of the myths about ADHD and see that a small set of actionable strategies can make all the difference, it's natural that you'll want to help others to do the same … and this is your chance.

Simply by sharing your honest opinion of this book and a little about your own experience, you'll help new readers achieve their goals and enrich their personal and work relationships.

TAKE A MOMENT TO SHARE YOUR THOUGHTS!

Thank you so much for your support. Your words are more powerful than you realize.

Scan the QR code to leave your review!

Conclusion

Over the past 15 chapters, you've been on an incredible journey of self-discovery through the lens of ADHD. It's become clear that having ADHD isn't something to figure out like a puzzle but rather a unique perspective that adds richness to your life. Your path with ADHD is full of potential and amazing qualities, and this book has given you the tools to unlock it.

The main message is simple: ADHD is a gift, not a burden. It gives you boundless energy, endless creativity, and a special way of thinking that can lead to remarkable achievements. The key is not to change who you are but to fully embrace it. Throughout these chapters, you've explored practical strategies that you can actually use in your daily life. Your journey with ADHD is an ongoing exploration, and applying what you've learned is the key to making progress.

As you've gone through these chapters, you've discovered valuable lessons that can truly transform your life. One important lesson is that hyperfocus is not a problem to fix but a superpower you can use for productivity and creativity. You've also learned the importance of being kind to yourself and understanding that mistakes and setbacks are opportunities for growth. Plus, you've gained insights into how mindfulness can help manage ADHD symptoms and improve focus.

Another important lesson is the power of community. You've seen how connecting with others who understand your experiences can provide invaluable support and a sense of belonging. And you've learned how advocating for yourself and the ADHD community can make a positive impact by dispelling myths and misconceptions.

These lessons aren't just theories; they're practical tools for creating a fulfilling and empowered life with ADHD. They're the building blocks for your journey toward success and personal growth. Your unique perspective and talents have the power to shape a world that embraces diversity and celebrates individuality. So, take these lessons to heart and continue your journey with confidence, knowing that you are destined for greatness.

In conclusion, remember this: ADHD is not an obstacle; it's a unique way of being extraordinary. Your journey with ADHD is full of potential and greatness. So, step out into the world with confidence, knowing that you have the tools and knowledge to thrive. At the same time, embrace your uniqueness, harness your superpowers, and continue your journey with curiosity and resilience.

Embrace Your Uniqueness: The most important lesson is to embrace your uniqueness. ADHD isn't the same for everyone; it's a spectrum, and you are at the heart of it. Your ADHD is as unique as your fingerprint. Embrace it, celebrate it, and let it shine. Your individuality is your greatest asset.

Harness Your Superpowers: Think of your ADHD as a superpower. You have endless energy, limitless creativity, and the ability to hyperfocus like a laser beam. Use them to your advantage and direct them towards your goals. Your exceptional strengths set you apart in remarkable ways.

Stay Curious and Keep Learning: Cultivate curiosity; it's your closest ally. Keep exploring, learning, and evolving. Whether it's through books, courses, or conversations, never stop nourishing your curious mind. Your insatiable curiosity is the driving force behind your personal and professional growth. Just think about the things you can achieve when you keep curious and use your hyperfocus to excel at anything you set your mind to!

Connect with Your Tribe: Remember the power of community. Surround yourself with people who understand and support you. Seek out ADHD support groups, both online and in your local community. Share your experiences, learn from others, and build meaningful connections. Your tribe is a source of encouragement and camaraderie on your ADHD journey.

Take Care of Your Well-being: Prioritize your mental and physical well-being; it's the foundation of your success. Make self-care a priority, get enough sleep, eat nourishing foods, and engage in regular physical activity. A healthy mind and body are your secret weapons, giving you the resilience and vitality to overcome challenges.

Embrace Setbacks as Stepping Stones: Remember that setbacks aren't failures; they are opportunities for growth. When faced with challenges, see them as stepping stones on your path to success. Learn from your experiences, adjust your strategies, and keep moving forward. Your ability to bounce back shows your resilience.

Be an Advocate for Empathy and Understanding: Champion empathy and understanding. Educate those around you about ADHD, dispelling myths and misconceptions. Create an environment where individuals with ADHD are accepted and supported. Your advocacy contributes to a more inclusive world for everyone.

As you continue your journey with ADHD, know that a bright future awaits. Yes, there might be some stormy clouds once in a while. But each day contributes to your growth, learning, and evolution. Your unique perspective and talents have the power to shape a world that embraces diversity and celebrates individuality.

Use the tools and insights you've gained from this book to lead a fulfilling, empowered life with ADHD. Don't just survive; thrive by consistently applying these strategies and embracing a community that supports you. Your journey is a testament to your strength, resilience, and limitless potential.

Thank you for joining me on this adventure. Your story is still a work in progress, and it's a story of triumph and inspiration. Embrace your ADHD, embrace yourself, and venture into the world with confidence, knowing that you are destined for greatness.

As we say goodbye for now, and if this book has been helpful to you, please consider leaving a review to share your thoughts and experiences. Your review can guide others on their ADHD journey and inspire them to embark on now of their own. By sharing your feedback, you contribute to a community of support and empowerment for those who see the world the way you do and have the potential to change someone else's life.

With heartfelt gratitude and best wishes,

Chelsi

References

ADDA Editorial Team. (2022, October 4). *The Challenges of Parenting with ADHD.* ADDA - Attention Deficit Disorder Association. https://add.org/parenting-challenges-with-adhd/

ADDitude Editors. (2017, March 14). *What Is ADHD? Everything You Need to Know.* ADDitude; ADDitude. https://www.additudemag.com/what-is-adhd-symptoms-causes-treatments/

ADHD Collective. ADHD Quotes for Information and Inspiration.Accessed January 4, 2024. https://adhdcollective.com/adhd-quotes-gallery/

Austin, R., & Pisano, G. (2017, July 18). *Neurodiversity Is a Competitive Advantage.* Harvard Business Review. https://hbr.org/2017/05/neurodiversity-as-a-competitive-advantage

Bailey, E. (2017, May 4). *Born This Way: Personal Stories of Life with ADHD.* ADDitude. https://www.additudemag.com/adhd-personal-stories-real-life-people-living-with-adhd/

Baumer, N., & Frueh, J. (2021, November 23). *What is neurodiversity?* Harvard Health Publishing. https://www.health.harvard.edu/blog/what-is-neurodiversity-202111232645

Bautista-González, M., A. (2023, October 18). *Cash, Overspending, and ADHD.* Cash Essentials. https://cashessentials.org/cash-impulse-spending-and-adhd/#:

Burch, K. (2022, January 7). *What Are Benefits of Having ADHD?* Verywell Health. https://www.verywellhealth.com/benefits-of-adhd-strengths-and-superpowers-5210520

Carolina Wellness Psychiatry. (n.d.). *Benefits and Challenges of ADHD in Relationships: Carolina Wellness Psychiatry, PLLC: Psychiatrists.* Www.carolinawellnesspsychiatry.com. https://www.carolinawellnesspsychiatry.com/blog/benefits-and-challenges-of-adhd-in-relationships

CHADD. (n.d.). *ADHD and Stress.* CHADD. https://chadd.org/adhd-and-stress/#:

Cherry, K. (2022, September 20). *Why Cultivating a Growth Mindset Can Boost Your Success.* Verywell Mind. https://www.verywellmind.com/what-is-a-mindset-2795025

Connect Couples Therapy. (2022, April 27). *6 Steps to Navigate ADHD in Your Relationship*. Connect Couples Therapy & Marriage Counseling. https://connectcouplestherapy.com/6-steps-to-navigate-adhd-in-your-relationship/

Dr. Norman, C. (2022, November 7). *Emotional Regulation Tips For ADHD*. Mental Health. https://www.online-therapy.com/blog/emotional-regulation-tips-for-adhd/

Dweck, C. (2015, March 2). *Carol Dweck: A Summary of The Two Mindsets*. Farnam Street. https://fs.blog/carol-dweck-mindset/

Elizabeth, S. (2021, January 25). *How to Make a Self Care Calendar*. Creative and Ambitious. https://creativeandambitious.com/how-to-make-a-self-care-calendar/

Ellis, R. R. (2022, June 26). *Slideshow: Beyond Inattention: How ADHD May Be Affecting Your Life*. WebMD. https://www.webmd.com/add-adhd/ss/slideshow-adhd-life

Everyday Design. (n.d.). *FAQ: How can you break down large goals into smaller, more manageable steps? - Everyday Design*. Www.everyday.design. https://www.everyday.design/faqs/how-can-you-break-down-large-goals-into-smaller-more-manageable-steps

Fairbank, R. (2023, March 1). *An ADHD diagnosis in adulthood comes with challenges and benefits*. Apa.org. https://www.apa.org/monitor/2023/03/adult-adhd-diagnosis

Frampton, N. (2023, February 14). *Five benefits of dating someone with ADHD*. Qbtech. https://www.qbtech.com/blog/five-benefits-of-dating-someone-with-adhd/

Giwerc, D. (n.d.). *Identify Your Strengths and Make Them Stronger*. Addca.com. Retrieved November 29, 2023, from https://addca.com/adhd-coach-training/ADHD-Blog-Details/identify_your_strengths_and_make_them_stronger/#:

Grcevich, S. (2010, September 24). *ADHD and Spiritual Disciplines*. Church4EveryChild. https://church4everychild.org/2010/09/24/adhd-and-spiritual-disciplines/

Gupta, S. (2023, November 20). *Coping With Mood Swings in ADHD*. Verywell Mind. https://www.verywellmind.com/mood-swings-in-adhd-symptoms-causes-and-coping-5223511#:

Hennah. (n.d.). *Impulsive Decision-Making*. Goally Apps & Tablets for Kids.

Retrieved December 16, 2023, from https://getgoally.com/blog/neurodi
versopedia/impulsive-decision-making/

Harvard | School of Public Health. (2013, November 4). *Make exercise a daily habit – 10 tips.* The Nutrition Source. https://www.hsph.harvard.edu/nutri
tionsource/2013/11/04/making-exercise-a-daily-habit-10-tips/#:

Hello Klarity. (2021, December 15). *Time Management For ADHD Adults: 11 Tips.* Www.helloklarity.com. https://www.helloklarity.com/post/time-
management-adhd-adults/

Hogan, L. (2019, March 6). *Roleplaying Difficult Conversations | Lara Hogan.* Larahogan.me. https://larahogan.me/blog/practice-difficult-conversa
tions/

Honos-Webb, L. (2021, July 9). 6 Secrets to Goal Setting with ADHD. *ADDitude.* https://www.additudemag.com/achieving-personal-goals-
adhd/#:

Huges, L. (2023, April 6). *Why are people with ADHD so unorganized?* Www.getinflow.io. https://www.getinflow.io/post/adhd-disorganization-tips

Hughes, L. (2023, January 29). *4 communication problems in ADHD relationships (and how to fix them).* Www.getinflow.io. https://www.getinflow.io/post/fix-
communication-problems-in-adhd-relationships

Illiades, C. (2013, October 10). *7 Favorite Fitness Tips for Adults With ADHD.* EverydayHealth.com. https://www.everydayhealth.com/adhd-pictures/
favorite-fitness-tips-for-adults-with-adhd.aspx

InnerDrive. (n.d.). *The benefits of a growth mindset, explained.* Blog.innerdrive.-
co.uk. https://blog.innerdrive.co.uk/benefits-of-growth-mindset-explained

Irish, J. (2023, March 20). *3 to-do list apps that actually work with ADHD | Zapier.* Zapier.com. https://zapier.com/blog/adhd-to-do-list/

Kagan, J. (2022, January 3). *Individual Retirement Account (IRA).* Investopedia. https://www.investopedia.com/terms/i/ira.asp

Kelly, K. (n.d.). *ADHD and Creativity.* Www.understood.org. https://www.under
stood.org/en/articles/adhd-and-creativity-what-you-need-to-know

LaPonsie, M. (2023, November 8). *9 Best Budget Apps.* U.S. News. https://
money.usnews.com/money/personal-finance/saving-and-budgeting/
slideshows/best-budget-apps

Leonard, J. (2019, May 31). *ADHD diet: Best foods, foods to avoid, and meal plans.* Www.medicalnewstoday.com. https://www.medicalnewstoday.com/arti
cles/325352#foods-to-limit-or-avoid

Loos, G. (2023, June 20). *Do You Know What Triggers Your ADHD Symptoms?* Psycom. https://www.psycom.net/adhd/adhd-symptom-triggers

Lovering, N. (2022, May 18). *ADHD and Emotions: Relationship and Tips to Manage.* Healthline. https://www.healthline.com/health/adhd/emotional-regulation#takeaway

Mandriota, M. (2022, April 6). *ADHD in Women vs. Men: How Prevalence and Symptoms Differ by Gender.* Psych Central. https://psychcentral.com/adhd/adhd-and-gender#recap

Martin, R. (2022, January 12). *50 tips for improving your emotional intelligence.* Www.rochemartin.com. https://www.rochemartin.com/blog/50-tips-improving-emotional-intelligence

Mayo Clinic. (2023, January 25). *Adult Attention-Deficit/Hyperactivity Disorder (ADHD) - Symptoms and Causes.* Mayo Clinic; Mayo Clinic. https://www.mayoclinic.org/diseases-conditions/adult-adhd/symptoms-causes/syc-20350878

McMillen, M. (2022, July 13). *Parenting When You Have ADHD.* WebMD. https://www.webmd.com/add-adhd/parenting-with-adhd

Mentalhelp.net. (2019, June 17). ADHD Comorbidity. *MentalHelp.* https://www.mentalhelp.net/adhd/and-comorbidity/

Miller, C. (2016, February 18). *ADHD and Exercise.* Child Mind Institute; Child Mind Institute. https://childmind.org/article/adhd-and-exercise/

Miller, C. (2023, April 21). *What Is Neurodiversity?* Child Mind Institute. https://childmind.org/article/what-is-neurodiversity/

Mio. (2023, September 11). *The Benefits of Neurodiversity in the Workplace.* Outbound Recruiting AI-Powered Platform | HireEZ. https://hireez.com/blog/neurodiversity-in-the-workplace/

Morin, A. (n.d.). *Amanda Morin | Understood.* Www.understood.org. https://www.understood.org/people/72f4882b3d364f64b32cacbc9aa051ba

Nall, R. (2021, January 19). *The Benefits of ADHD.* Healthline; Healthline Media. https://www.healthline.com/health/adhd/benefits-of-adhd#what-the-research-says

Niemiec, R. (n.d.). *A Mindful Pause To Change Your Day | VIA Institute.* Www.viacharacter.org. https://www.viacharacter.org/topics/articles/a-mindful-pause-to-change-your-day

Nwogwugwu, S. (2022, October 1). *Sussan Nwogwugwu | Profile.* EI Magazine. https://www.ei-magazine.com/profile/sussan-nwogwugwu/profile

One Bright Mental Health. (2023, February 16). *Lesser-Known Symptoms of*

ADHD in Adults. Onebright. https://onebright.com/advice-hub/news/undiagnosed-adhd-lesser-known-symptoms-adhd/

Pacheco, D. (2022, April 29). *ADHD and Sleep Problems: How Are They Related?* Sleep Foundation. https://www.sleepfoundation.org/mental-health/adhd-and-sleep

Pant, P. (2022, June 20). *What is the difference between wants and needs?* The Balance. https://www.thebalancemoney.com/how-to-separate-wants-and-needs-453592

Paula. (2022, September 12). *How Do I Accept My ADHD Diagnosis?* I'm Busy Being Awesome. https://imbusybeingawesome.com/accept-adhd-diagnosis/

Pettit, M. (2020, March 4). *The Importance of Writing Down Your Goals - Lucemi Consulting.* Lucemi Consulting: Productivity and Time Management Coach. https://lucemiconsulting.co.uk/writing-down-your-goals/#:

Primary Health Care-The Project. (2017, December 18). *The Importance of Social Support | The Project.* Phctheproject.org. https://phctheproject.org/the-importance-of-social-support/

Roybal, B. (2008, May 13). *ADHD Diet and Nutrition.* WebMD; WebMD. https://www.webmd.com/add-adhd/adhd-diets

Saline, S. (2022, February 3). *ADHD and Self-Awareness | Psychology Today.* Www.psychologytoday.com. https://www.psychologytoday.com/intl/blog/your-way-adhd/202202/adhd-and-self-awareness

Scott, E. (2010, March 8). *Types of Social Support.* Verywell Mind; Verywellmind. https://www.verywellmind.com/types-of-social-support-3144960

Sherrel, Z. (2021, September 20). *ADHD and procrastination: Impact and management.* Www.medicalnewstoday.com. https://www.medicalnewstoday.com/articles/adhd-procrastination#:

Smith, J. (2020, September 25). *Growth mindset vs fixed mindset: how what you think affects what you achieve.* Mindset Health. https://www.mindsethealth.com/matter/growth-vs-fixed-mindset

Special Strong. (2023, November 9). *The Best Exercise for ADHD in Adults.* Special Strong. https://www.specialstrong.com/the-best-exercise-for-adhd-in-adults/

Stanton, T. (2023, July 23). *What are the benefits of neurodiversity for society as a whole?* Neurodiversity.guru. https://www.neurodiversity.guru/what-are-the-benefits-of-neurodiversity-for-society-as-a-whole

WebMD Editorial Contributors. (2022, September 20). *Attention Deficit Hyperactivity Disorder (ADHD)*. WebMD. https://www.webmd.com/add-adhd/attention-deficit-hyperactivity-disorder-adhd

York, A. (2023, July 31). *The 10 Best ADHD Apps to Stay on Top of Your Day*. ClickUp. https://clickup.com/blog/adhd-apps/

Made in the USA
Coppell, TX
12 November 2024

40085286R00138